You Can't Teach
THROUGH A

**And
Other
Epiphanies
for
Educators**

MARVIN W. BERKOWITZ

You Can't Teach Through a Rat and Other Epiphanies for Educators
by Marvin W. Berkowitz

Publisher: Character Development Group, Inc.
366 Bella Vista Dr., Boone, NC 28607
Toll-free: 888.262.0572
Email: Info@CharacterEducation.com
www.CharacterEducation.com

ISBN: 1-892056-56-9

Printed in the United States of America

$16.95

Dedication

This book is dedicated to the memory of
Sanford Noyes McDonnell (1922-2012)
who gave me the opportunity to work with, learn from,
and love all the educators who have inspired this book.

Table of Contents

Introduction

A Confession

This book is for educators.

But I need to offer a confession before we go any further.

I am not a teacher. Well, that is not exactly true. I have been teaching, after all, for nearly 40 years, but all of my teaching has been at the post-secondary level. I have taught full-time at universities (mainly in the Department of Psychology at Marquette University and the College of Education at the University of Missouri–St. Louis) since 1979, part-time at a host of other institutions prior to that while getting my doctoral and post-doctoral training, and as a visiting scholar sporadically throughout my career.

But I have never taught elementary, middle, or high school students. Well, except for a few guest appearances.

To make matters worse, I am not, by training, an educator. My undergraduate, masters and doctoral degrees are all in psychology. And the bulk of my career has been spent teaching and studying child and adolescent development in psychology departments. Other than my post-doctoral work at the Harvard Graduate School of Education and my sabbatical studies, my current position as the Sanford N. McDonnell Professor of Character Education is my first real trial as a full-time member of an education unit at a university.

Juergen Habermas, a brilliant and creative scholar from Germany, once wrote a book entitled *Legitimation Crisis*. He was referring to a management class that had no legitimacy in the eyes of the workers they managed, largely because they had not risen from the worker ranks to management. He saw this as a trend. Well I have worried about my own legitimation crisis ever since formally entering the field of education in my current position. Do I have legitimacy to advise elementary, middle and high school teachers and administrators? Over the past decade, I have found that educators accept me, seem to like what I have to say, and tend to find that my advice, perspective and training are of use to them as they navigate the immensely challenging terrain of educating and socializing youth in schools. Well, most of them...but that is another story and more a matter of flaws in my character (e.g., hubris and tactlessness) than flaws in my message.

But the old anxieties about my legitimacy reappeared when I considered the audacious task of writing a book in which I, as a relative outsider to the world of education, intended to tell educators how to think differently about what they do. And that is precisely the purpose of this book...to help educators identify some common trouble spots in maximizing the positive impact of schools on student learning and development.

Fortunately for me (and hopefully for you as well), I have two factors working in my favor. One, I tend to be overly confident about the validity of my ideas. So my trepidations fall far short of being sufficient to daunt me and deter me from the task. Two, I firmly believe that the emperor has an enduring tendency to walk around buck naked. And I relish pointing it out to those who don't seem to notice it. Fresh eyes often see what those in the inner circle miss, a theme that is explored in Chapter 9.

When I walk into schools or listen to educators, I often wonder why they do what they do or say what they say. And often why they do what they do when they say what they say. And why they don't seem to see the inconsistencies, irrationalities, illogic, and inaccuracies around them.

The Emperor Has No Clothes

Recently Tatiana Golikova, a visiting scholar from Russia who was spending her Fulbright fellowship to study and work with us at the Center for Character and Citizenship, joined me at a presentation about a wonderful middle school (Halifax Middle School, Halifax, PA), which had achieved true excellence by rethinking schooling and transforming it to support the education and development of the whole child, largely around a set of character outcomes. Bob Hassinger, the pioneering former principal of Halifax Middle (and now the superintendent of the district) was doing a marvelous job of presenting the school as a caring, student-centered, value- and purpose-driven school. One of the slides he presented led Tatiana to ask why the list of caring virtues that were foundational to the school's mission and purpose was accompanied by a caricature of a feral beast.

Bob appeared confused, as did most of the rest of audience. The school mascot is the "Wildcat" and that logo was on the slide. But many schools have such mascots and fail to reflect on what they represent. In Russia, schools don't have mascots, so it was quite salient to Tatiana. I have often chided schools for absurd mascots. Once while in an elementary school in the middle of a full day in-service workshop for the staff, we moved to the gymnasium for an activity. I noticed the decorations and said to the teachers, "I see that your mascot is the pirate" to which they collectively nodded and grinned. My response was "nice choice for an elementary school, to choose as a mascot a raping, pillaging, murdering criminal." They were stunned. They had never even considered the meaning and implications of their mascot.

As a developmental psychologist, I see schools and classrooms through the lens of what supports healthy child development; and that perspective is needed to inform good educational practice.

Intentional Discomfort

Whenever I provide professional development to educators (or anyone for that matter), I routinely tell, or should I say warn, the participants that I have three broad goals: to *inform*; to *inspire*; and to *disconcert*. The first goal is ubiquitous and the second common. But the last is anomalous and hence takes most people by surprise. However, just as weightlifters and bodybuilders claim "no pain, no gain," developmental psychologists can argue that there is "no development without conflict and discomfort." That is admittedly a bit of an overstatement, but the point is that entering your *discomfort zone* is often necessary to make substantial progress.

My friend and colleague, Hal Urban (a former high school teacher and author of a wonderful book, *Lessons from the Classroom*) did not let his students "park" in their comfort zone. Reasonable risk-taking is necessary for growth. I have had many job titles through the years, but I have come to believe that I should print new business cards with one title on it: *Epiphany Engineer*. As I have worked with educators, I have come to recognize that perhaps my most helpful contribution is to be a catalyst for their epiphanies; to shake their foundations and get them to take a new fresh look at their practices and their calling. And I have found numerous "sticking points";

that is, particular practices and insights that seem particularly hard to budge for many educators.

That is why I wrote this book. I want to help educators rethink what they are doing to, with, and for children. I want them to feel a bit uncomfortable about how they currently understand schools, the purposes of education, what it means to be a professional and a colleague, and what really helps children learn and grow. If I fail at that, then I have failed in the fundamental purpose for writing this book.

This book could not have been written without all the teachers in my life. After all, I did not study education. I experienced it. For the past 13 years full time and part-time for a long period prior to that, I have taught educators, and in the process they have taught me. So I thank all the teachers I have had, and, more importantly, I thank the literally thousands of teachers and principals whom I have taught and worked with, especially over the past decade in St. Louis. These are educators who thirst for a better way of serving the students they teach. They have informed me, inspired me, and disconcerted me. Just I as I hope this book does for you.

Coda: A Word About the Title

When I proposed the title for this book, I unintentionally divided the world. It was quite a polarizing proposal. Some of my friends and colleagues loved it; others hated it, or at least strongly doubted the wisdom of trying to sell a book with a title like *You Can't Teach Through a Rat*. Understandably, no one knew what it meant. I never expected it to be self-explanatory and I am not going to preface this book by explaining it here. You will know what it means when you read the chapter by the same title, and if you just have to know, read Chapter 2 first.

This is a book of 20 discrete epiphanies and one of them centers on the title of the book. I thought of highly popular books like Oliver Sacks's *The Man Who Mistook His Wife for a Hat: And Other Clinical Tales* and the more recent and wildly successful *Freakonomics: A Rogue Economist Explores the Hidden Side of Everything* by Steven Levitt and Stephen Dubner. Their cryptic titles, even with negative connotations like "freak" or "mistook his wife" didn't seem to impede their success, and that is precisely the kind of criticism I received from those friends and colleagues who thought a more straightforward and positive title would be preferable. They feared that people would see the title and shy away from or simply not understand the book. I have much more faith in the undying, albeit sometimes imprudent, curiosity endemic to basic human nature.

The other concern was that the word "epiphany" would be either unfamiliar or uninterpretable to most readers. I think that most people have heard it, but perhaps most are not fully familiar with its meaning. According to the Merriam-Webster online dictionary, an epiphany is "a usually sudden manifestation or perception of the essential nature or meaning of something; (2) an intuitive grasp of reality through something (as an event) usually simple and striking; (3) an illuminating discovery, realization, or disclosure." It is based on the New Testament event of the Magi discovering Christ, and is now celebrated as a holiday on January 6. In fact, another meaning of the word is "an appearance or manifestation especially of a divine being" however I want to be clear that I am making no such claims here, although many of my students and friends might accuse me of such.

So if the title was off-putting or otherwise less than helpful to you, I apologize. I used it because I liked it. I hope you will too, or will come to do so after reading the book. If not, ignore it and read on!

A Word of Thanks

This book was vastly improved by the wonderful feedback I received from a few generous souls who took the time to read an early draft and suggest improvements. I want to thank Tom Lickona, Hal Urban, Phil Vincent, Danny Berkowitz, Beatrice Shivers, Wolfgang Althof, Diane Stirling, Amy Johnston, Clifton Taulbert, Mary Anne Hoppe, and Dick Chudnow. Each brought a different lens to the book and helped me to improve it in so many important ways.

On Purpose

We have lost our way in American education. For centuries, education was understood to have multiple interlocking purposes. One purpose was, and is, the transmission of knowledge and fostering of academic competencies. Schools have always taught things. Such things may be language proficiency, the competencies to manipulate numbers, knowledge of the history and principles of one's (or others') culture, and appreciation for and proficiency in the arts.

I have two fundamental questions about this focus on the teaching of things. The first is "why?" Why have we taught children these things in school? What is the justification to have schools that teach such things?

Now you may think this a silly question. But there is a great study that responds to a parallel question asked of parents: "Why do parents choose to have children?" The results are fascinating. There are many answers. Sometimes it is for love of children. Sometimes it is to continue a family lineage. Sometimes it is to fulfill one's own need to be loved. Sometimes it is simply for biological reasons (sex, after all, is pleasurable). Sometimes it is for economic or political reasons. Interestingly, the reasons given tend to differ in different cultures.

So if the question is good enough for parenting, it ought to be good enough for teaching. What is the reason we have schools for children and adolescents? We need to think about why education focuses so heavily on teaching kids things. There is a concept in psychology called functional autonomy. Once you do something long enough, it becomes its own reason for existing, independent of why you originally began doing it. I think that has happened in education. We began teaching kids things for a reason (or reasons) and now we do it...well, just because.

Clearly, we teach kids things so that they will know these particular things. Of course this raises the question of why we think they need to know *those* particular things, rather than other things we don't teach (or spend less time on). And that opens up quite a can of worms. In an economically-based culture like the U.S. one of the large worms in the can is that knowing "things" has economic value. At least knowing some things does. And schools tend to focus on the things that have economic value (like literacy, science, and math).

The second question is "is this the only purpose of schooling?" Are schools here mainly or only to prepare kids to be workers? To generate capital? I would argue that this is not the only purpose of schooling. In fact, I would argue that teaching things so that we can work is a lesser purpose of education. Of course, we also teach things—such as appreciating beautiful music, great literature, and the lessons of history—that have less likelihood of impacting one's place in the market, but it is patently clear that they have less status in our educational system. Also when the pressure builds—because of economic downturns, falling behind other nations in educational statistics or market share, etc.—the humanities, arts, physical education, and character education are the first to be cut.

> For as long as people have been educating youth, a primary function was socialization. It was intended to prepare the next generation to responsibly inherit and shepherd and take care of society.

Primary Purpose of Education

Fortunately, I am in good company in critiquing this mentality. In fact, many of the founders of this society argued strongly that a primary purpose of education was to prepare future citizens of our (then) daring and fledgling experiment in democratic self-governance. And then there was the concern in the early part of the 20th century that the vagabond children of new immigrants were running amok in the streets of our cities. Compulsory universal education was in part justified as a way to deal with the children of immigrants; that is, to transform them from an urban nuisance (or even criminal class) into productive citizens.

For as long as people have been educating youth, a primary function was socialization. It was intended to prepare the next generation to responsibly inherit and shepherd and take care of society. We pass down knowledge of the culture so that it will not be lost, whether through the oral traditions of many aboriginal cultures or through the textbooks of contemporary schools. We teach literacy and numeracy so that they can effectively manage the society. We teach appreciation of the arts and humanities so that the best that we have created will be treasured, preserved, and expanded. And we simply teach them how to be with others, for society, after all, is a matter of being with others. Education, which has long been the guarantor of societal preservation, has instead sadly devolved into a simple and narrow matter of workforce development.

How Did We Get Where We Are?

How did this happen? It is complicated, but a few major factors are worth noting here. About half a century ago, two major events led to changes in education and how we viewed it, changes that generated a misguided and myopic view of its purpose. First was the move to legislate and enforce the separation of religion from public schooling. Mind you, I am not arguing that worship or proselytizing should be brought back into public schools. And I wholeheartedly support the First Amendment's prohibition of the government's establishing a religion; in fact, I think it was brilliant of the founders of this nation to make this such a priority. Furthermore, it is important to recognize that the first amendment of the U.S. Constitution does not preclude any presence of religion in schools; rather it just precludes the advocacy of religious beliefs in public schools.

My point here, however, is different. Values and morality were so closely tied to religion in our society, that the mid-20th century legislation about prohibiting religious teaching in public schools led to what essentially was throwing out the baby (values, ethics, morality, character) with the bathwater (religious worship and advocacy in public schools). People considered, and some often still consider, religion as synonymous with morality, despite the fact that ethical philosophy has been around for millennia. Ethical philosophers, and regular folk, can think clearly and logically about matters of right and wrong without having to rely on religious justifications, as a moment's reflection makes clear.

For example, you can use religion as a basis in arguing against stealing, stating that it is a violation of one of the 10 Commandments. But using human reason, you can also argue that stealing is wrong because one would not want others stealing from them, or that if everyone stole then the world would be much less safe and desirable. You obviously don't have to be a trained moral philosopher to arrive at common-sense moral conclusions. In fact, even pre-schoolers make moral judgments whenever they claim that "it's not fair" (although that does not mean their moral assessment is accurate). Nor do you have to rely on religion to make such judgments.

The second event that steered us away from a rich and multifaceted understanding of the larger purposes of education—those transcending economic value—was the Soviets' successful launch of the Sputnik satellite in 1957. This was a deep shock to the American psyche, which had always assumed that the U.S. was first in science, technology, etc. A national panic over "losing the space race" resulted in an immediate call for more emphasis on math and science, turning some schools, especially high schools, into mini-technology universities. Social studies, values education, and other "soft" subjects took a back seat.

In the late 1960s and 1970s, a set of cultural events and upheavals (Vietnam War, the civil rights movement, the women's liberation movement, etc.) led to the re-entry of morality and values in the public schools in the form of "values clarification" and "moral education." The values clarification approach put the school in a neutral position of just asking students to "clarify" whatever their values happened to be. A colleague shared that one eighth-grade teacher, asking her kids each to list "what you love to do," found that their top-ranked items were "sex, drugs, and rock and roll." Understandably, values clarification drew fire from many parents and also from scholars who pointed out its underlying moral relativism (all values were seen as equally good, to be freely chosen by the individual) and lack of any supporting empirical research, and was short-lived.

Moral education, a much smaller movement, lasted longer but its focus was narrowly on one part of character; that is, on fostering the development of critical thinking about social and moral issues.

During the 1970s, the "open classroom" movement, originating in Britain, found traction in many American schools as an alternative to the Sputnik-inspired math-and-science focus of the late 50s and early 60s. But because open education was often poorly implemented—emphasizing open archi-tecture (schools without walls between classrooms, for example) rather than a curriculum that was open to children's interests—this school reform even-tually triggered still another swing of the educational pendulum: the Back to Basics movement of the 1980s.

Fast forward to 2000 and the election of President George W. Bush. He had campaigned against "the soft bigotry of low expectations," correctly pointing out that many kids, especially minority students, were "socially promoted" through the grades and often graduated with little ability to read, write, or calculate and therefore little ability to get and keep a job. To correct this edu-cational inequity, Bush implemented what I like to call "the new Sputnik"... the federal No Child Left Behind (NCLB) legislation, which is once again narrowing the purpose and scope of education.

Defenders of NCLB cite increased school accountability for the learning of all student sub-groups and some evidence of improved test scores, but this "solution" soon created a host of new problems. Reading and math quickly gobbled up most of the school day; subjects such as science, social studies, music, and art got less time and funding; goals such as creativity and criti-cal thinking moved to the back burner; principals feared that they would, because of inadequate "annual yearly progress" for all sub-groups, end up on the "in need of improvement" or "failing schools" list; teachers therefore began to teach to the test; and school became a much more stressful, joyless, and educationally impoverished place for kids and teachers alike. All of this is amply documented and thoughtfully discussed in educational historian Diane Ravitch's 2010 book, *The Death and Life of The Great American School System*. Once a supporter of No Child Left Behind, Ravitch is now one of its strongest critics.

In short, in the current educational climate of No Child Left Behind and high-stakes testing, education has again become narrow in scope and dis-connected from its history and rich purpose. We have once again forgot-ten why we educate our youth, and we have become fixated on the idea of schools—even elementary schools—as college preparatory and workforce development institutions. Pedagogy has devolved in a parallel and derivative way. A metaphor for our current approach to teaching is a semi-automatic pedagogical BB gun. The BBs are factoids. Upon being certified, it is as if teachers are issued their own metaphorical pedagogical BB gun (pre-service teacher education) and equipped with a supply of BBs (subject knowledge) or at least access to the ammo (curricula). The new pedagogical goal is to shoot as many factoid BBs into the brains of children as they can in the limited time they have access to them in school. The assumption seems to be that getting factoids into brains is the greatest purpose of education.

> Ultimately a primary academic goal is for students to learn how to learn and to come to want to learn. In this age of technology, most students can learn anytime and anyplace...if they know how and want to. And more and more students will have this access in the future.

What Matters Most in Education

But education has multiple purposes, and academic learning is only one of them. Furthermore, quantity of facts is far from the richest form of academic learning. Most of the factoids we learn in school are arbitrary. Certainly we need to be literate and competent at basic mathematics, etc. But whether we learn about Fort Sumpter or another battle is really of little import. Or memorizing the order of chemical symbols in the Table of Elements. And so on. Ultimately a primary academic goal is for students to learn how to learn and to come to want to learn. In this age of technology, most students can learn anytime and anyplace...if they know how and want to. And more and more students will have this access in the future.

Dating back to the classical Greeks, it has been recognized that a self-governing society cannot endure if its citizens are not virtuous. This was repeatedly and resoundingly reinforced by the shapers of our great experiment in democracy, including Thomas Jefferson, Benjamin Franklin, and James Monroe. Alexis deToqueville came to the U.S. from Europe in the mid-19th century to figure out in part how Americans, comprised largely of groups with quite diverse and often extreme religious perspectives, were succeeding in building a society out of wilderness through a self-governing democracy, and without an aristocracy or cultural history. He concluded that a major secret to our success was that we were successful because of our core societal and personal values. And he warned that if we ceased to be value-driven, we would cease to flourish. The founders as well as observers like de Toqueville knew that the survival of the United States of America depended on the positive values of its citizens, and they further recognized that education was a critical force in shaping those values. Schools are not just there to feed the economy; they are there to sustain and nurture the culture, the political system, the entire society.

> Schools are not just there to feed the economy; they are there to sustain and nurture the culture, the political system, the entire society.

Of course, I don't want to imply that America has been built only on positive values or that all Americans, then or now, held only positive values. When my son read the above paragraph, he cautioned me that America was also built upon "genocide of the indigenous population and an economy powered by chattel slavery." We freely accepted many immoral policies and institutions, oppressing many groups (women, children, minorities, immigrants, Native Americans, etc.) and individuals. But the positive value strands (democracy, individual human rights, Judeo-Christian morality, etc.) were the underpinnings of much of the success of this nation.

The Power of Purpose

As we grapple with the purposes of education, it may help to take a detour for a moment and think about purpose more broadly. Bill Damon, Director of the Stanford University Center on Adolescence, has been a leader in the formation of a new focus in developmental psychology, that of *adolescent purpose*. He argues that adolescence is prime developmental territory for grappling with such existential questions as one's purpose on this earth. He and now many others are studying this question and designing programs for adolescent students to reflect on and craft a sense of their own purpose. When teens have a strong sense of purpose, they are more likely to flourish and less likely to engage in behaviors that harm self and others. When Hal Urban, author of *Lessons from the Classroom*, was still teaching high school, he assigned his students the task of writing a personal mission statement, an idea borrowed from Stephen Covey's *The 7 Habits of Highly Effective People*. The John Templeton Foundation's Laws of Life essay contest asks students to write essays about a core value around which they wish to live their lives.

This individual focus on purpose has a parallel in broader educational philosophy and policy. A recent international study of education by Mark Tucker and his colleagues (see their book *Surpassing Shanghai*) gleaned ideas to improve U.S. education by looking at other nations that were leaving us in the educational dust. While finding many helpful practices, they also focused on purpose. Many other highly successful nations (in terms of educational outcomes)—Diane Ravitch cites Finland as a prime example—understood or were beginning to emphasize the importance of educating, not just for academic success, but also to support the core values of their society. I was recently in China, which is at a cultural crossroads of sorts, and it was clear that many were grappling with which value cluster should undergird education and particularly educational reform. Should they hang on to Communist era values, move to more democratic and/or market-driven values, or return to more classical values (e.g., Confucianism)?

It is not just nations that have to grapple with the question of core values and purpose in education. In their recent study of high-performing schools and their leaders (*Getting it Done*), Karin Chenoweth and Kristina Theokas concluded that such leaders "use their core beliefs about the deep purpose of education and the capacity of all students to motivate their staffs and sustain their own courage and stamina in the face of obstacles." Purpose is critical, and it is clearly more than academic success. So how can we identify the other purposes of education?

The "Civic Mission of Schools"

Productive citizens are not simply smart people who have lots of BBs in their brains (know lots of facts) and can reason in abstract and impressive ways. They also have the skills and mindset (dispositions, values, virtues) necessary for democratic citizenship. In other words, they have civic character. This includes a commitment to the common good, a willingness to enter the public sphere and debate political and ethical issues, and the skills necessary for learning about, intellectually digesting, and responding publicly to societal issues and challenges. They need to care about the common good, feel and take responsibility for shepherding it and the society that protects it, and understand the necessity of citizenship for the survival of society. As is described in Chapter 19, they also need the inclination and capacity for responsible dissent.

Schools must be places where this knowledge, these skills, and these dispositions form and flourish. Students, however, don't develop civic character merely by learning *about* citizenship, government, and democracy. They develop it by *experiencing* democracy, by experiencing the power of their voices in the common sphere, and by being given responsibility for the common good. Shooting factoids into brains does not do that. A second major purpose of schools, beyond the academic purpose, is fostering civic character, and that has great implications for *what* we teach, but even more importantly for *how* we teach what we teach.

Moral and Performance Character

I have argued thus far that schools exist not only to promote academic learning but also to promote civic character. But that is still not all. The traits of civic character, important as they are, are not all that makes one a good person. The flourishing of all societies ultimately depends on the moral character of their citizens. So a third and related purpose of education is the general moral and character development of students. Whereas moral and civic character are not mutually exclusive concepts, they are also not the same thing. Civic character refers to those characteristics of the person that motivate and enable him or her to responsibly and effectively participate in the political and public sphere—public defense of one's idea, critical evaluation of political messages, responsible dissent, etc. Moral character refers to those characteristics of the person that motivate and enable him or her to do the ethically right thing—honesty, integrity, respect for persons, compassion, etc.

> The job of socializing all citizens must begin in childhood and is the responsibility of all societal institutions, including the schools.

The job of socializing all citizens must begin in childhood and is the responsibility of all societal institutions, including the schools. Beyond those three purposes, to be able to put one's knowledge, civic character, and moral character into effective use, one needs what Tom Lickona and Matt Davidson, in their book *Smart and Good High Schools*, have dubbed *performance character*. In the Character Education Partnership's position paper (*Performance Values:*

Why They Matter and What Schools Can Do to Foster Their Development),
performance character is defined as qualities that "enable us to achieve, given
a supportive environment, our highest potential in any performance context
(the classroom, the athletic arena, the workplace, etc.)."

> **The Four Purposes of Education**
> • Academic Learning
> • Civic Character, Knowledge and Skills
> • Moral Character and Knowledge
> • Performance Character and Skills

Knowledge, competence, *and* Integrity

You may be tempted to prioritize the four purposes of schools: academic
learning, civic character, performance character, and moral character. If you
are, I ask you to ponder something Samuel Johnson once wrote: "Integrity
without knowledge is weak and useless, and knowledge without integrity
is dangerous and dreadful." Think of it this way. Suppose you had to walk
through one of two doors, each leading to a different world. And it was one
way; no return. This was it for life. Suppose one door led to a world of igno-
rant but caring, ethical people. In this world everyone was a kind and gentle
soul, but no one had ever spent a day in school and none had ever learned
to read and hence had never read a book. There was no formal teaching and
they knew very little beyond what they had directly experienced in their
daily lives.

Suppose that in the other world everyone was highly educated and brilliant but selfish and antisocial. These people were incredibly clever and did
not care about anyone else. So which door would you choose?

I think it is a no-brainer. As Johnson noted, it is dangerous to educate
people without a moral compass, or as former President Teddy Roosevelt
once said, "To educate a person in mind and not in morals is to educate a
menace to society." This suggests that if you prioritize the purposes of education, it is dangerous to put academic achievement at the top.

Yet that is precisely what we have done in the U.S. for the past half century
at least. The same international comparative study of education that we dis-

cussed above (by Tucker) in regards to purpose also noted that much of what we have emphasized in U.S. educational policy does not exist in the practices and policies of those nations

that are far surpassing us in educational outcomes. We seem to be fixated on and invested in practices and policies that have no research base and are not present in cases of success.

We Are a Service Profession

Another way to think about this is to understand education as a service industry. Schools are there to serve children, and more importantly their development. Schools are not there to teach; they are there for children to learn...and to grow and flourish. Educators are in a service profession. We can easily think of schools as servants of society, and much of what I have just said fits that nicely. Indeed schools are partially there to serve society, but they are also there to serve their customers, their clients, their wards; that is, our children.

Sadly, this is often forgotten. Local school boards, teachers' unions, teachers themselves, often forget this central truth. Schools are not there for the adults. Rather the adults are there for schools and schools are there for the children.

There is a complex interplay undergirding the relationship of schools and children and society. On the one hand, schools educate and socialize children for the sake of the future of society. But our society exists to preserve the universal rights of its citizens. Remember life, liberty and the pursuit of happiness? Our democratic system exists to serve its citizens, but this only works if the citizens understand this as serving the common good of citizens and not simply one's personal interests. Likewise, schools are there to serve children who in turn need to come to recognize their responsibility to care for the common good and the society that, at least in theory, serves it.

One way to think about this comes from my friend and colleague Clifton Taulbert. In his book *Eight Habits of the Heart for Educators*, he talks about "seeing the possibilities" in children. The point is not to see an eight- or 18-year-old as he or she is currently, but to see the adult that child can become. Taulbert's claim is grounded in the fact that he became an internationally acclaimed author and speaker because people in the rural and then legally segregated Mississippi delta saw beyond the poor black child laborer to what he could become. Only because of that did he indeed realize his potential. Schools exist in large part to serve the possibilities in children.

The philosopher Bill Puka once introduced the concept of *developmental love*. This notion suggests that one form of love is serving the developmental needs of a child. Hal Urban defines character education simply as "bringing out the best in people." Developmental love then is showing one's love for a child by serving the development of the best possibilities in that child.

Why should we do that in general and in schools? The famous psycho-social theorist, Erik Erikson, said that the final piece of parenting is "to insure to [one's children] all of the stages of a healthy development." What he meant was that if one brings children into the world, ideally one is then obligated to serve the optimal development of that child. There is an obligation in parenting and it is service to the development of the child.

In a parallel fashion, if schools are to be charged with serving children, then they too must be obligated to serve the best developmental interests of the child. There is a profound difference between teachers who see their primary function as teaching subjects and teachers who see their primary function as teaching students. And in teaching students while serving their best interests, there is no higher interest than the formation of one's moral character. As we watch the escalation of interpersonal and global violence, it helps to think deeply about the kind of people our society is raising and educating. It is important to recognize that there are multiple purposes of education and that educating for character is paramount among them. After all, there is no future without children, but there is no moral future without children of character. And it is up to schools to contribute to this critical mission. We will live in a markedly better world if all educators take this to heart...on purpose.

> After all, there is no future without children, but there is no moral future without children of character.

You Can't Teach Through a Rat

Have you ever had the following student in your class?

Teacher: OK, please open your text books. Who can tell me where we left off yesterday?

Student (eagerly waving his hand).

Teacher: Yes, Chris.

Chris: My brother has a pet rat!

Of course you have had such a student. We all have. And I am not talking about a student who has a diagnosable reason for such behavior. I am just talking about a student who has something on his mind that is much more interesting to him or her than what is in the textbook that is about to be revisited by this class. It happens every day in every school. Furthermore, this may also occur in every class in all grade levels from kindergarten to graduate school!

Chris has an image of a rat firmly imprinted on his consciousness. This rat is sitting, front and center, on his cortex. To a student, seeing a rat in his brother's room is pretty darn intriguing...and memorable. This rat is sitting right on Chris's brain, just hovering there between you and Chris's cortex, and Chris is rather unlikely to learn math or language skills or anything else until that rat stops blocking the path to his cortex. That rat is sitting between Chris and what you want to teach him, but...*you simply can't teach through a rat.*

So, as a teacher (1) you need to know when there are rats in kids' brains and (2) you must have some effective means of removing those rats from kids' brains. There is no Pied Piper in your school or curriculum and I bet they didn't teach you rat removal in your teacher preparation education courses. Nonetheless, it is a critical skill for a teacher to have. You need it in your pedagogical arsenal. Otherwise you are spinning your wheels and frustrating your students by trying to teach through those rats.

Rat Removal Strategies

So what can you do? First, you have to come to the realization that students have lives. And that they do not check those lives at the door of your school or classroom. Sadly, this seems to be a fundamental subconscious assumption of schools; that is, that kids come to school ready to learn and that they leave their lives in their lockers, at the bus stop, or at home.

Unfortunately, kids actually have the audacity and inconsiderateness to bring their lives with them to school! And there is not much you can do about that. Metal detectors in school doorways (don't get me started!) do not neutralize or remove kids' lives as they enter the school portals. My friend and colleague, Phil Vincent, grew up in North Carolina and said that when hunting season began, kids would bring their shot guns to school and leave them in their vehicles on their gun racks (I know, I know. This seems unfathomable in our modern world). Even then the kids could leave their guns outside in their cars and focus on the work of schooling before they focused on the work of food-gathering after the school day ended, but they still couldn't leave their lives (and rats) out there, and kids today cannot do it either. (Interestingly, Phil also told me that you could get into trouble leaving the school grounds to eat lunch without a senior pass but not for bringing a shot gun to school in your car or truck on the gun rack. Times sure do change, eh?)

Just as teachers and principals bring their lives to school (more on this in Chapter 17), so do students. You know that there are days when you are under the weather, haven't slept well, or have some crisis going on in your personal life that is casting a shadow on your work day. It happens to everyone. Similarly, there are days when you are feeling especially chipper. Life is good and this shines the light of joy on your work day. Those shadows and clouds and rays of sunshine in your life affect how you function at work. On bad days your fuse is shorter and your demeanor a bit darker. On good days you are more tolerant, more fun, and more energetic. Students sense this.

They typically don't know why you are acting differently and treating them more or less fairly, but they surely notice that you are.

Well, it is no different for students. Just like Mary's little lamb from the popular children's song followed her to school each day, children's lives follow them to school each day. Unlike Mary's lamb or Phil's shotgun, however, their lives don't wait outside the school door. Instead they follow the students to their seats and affect their behavior. The lamb may wait outside the school for Mary, but Chris's rat follows him not only to school but right into the classroom, distracting him from school work. And it is not fair to blame a child because his father had a heart attack last night, or his mom gave birth to his baby sister early that morning, or the house next door had a fire last night, etc. It is also not fair to blame the child if there was no food in the house for breakfast. Or that her dad beat mom this morning or mom was arrested for selling drugs. Those "rats" are not their fault and are not readily left at the school door.

After you acknowledge the possibility that students may be thinking about something other than what you want them to focus on, the second thing you need to do is make peace with this notion and not vilify students for having lives that follow them to school. It is not their fault. It is just a fact of...well, life. If you are entitled to a life, so is every child in your class. And we can expect you to handle it better than a child can, can't we? So we have to cut them some slack on this one.

One of my doctoral students teaches in a large urban high school. When another of my doctoral students went to observe his class, he was stunned that so many of the students were sleeping at their desks throughout the first period class. He knew the teacher, his fellow student, well and knew he was a devoted and effective teacher. He was perplexed to see that he allowed his students to sleep through class. In fact, both of them had been highly influenced by Hal Urban and his educational wisdom based on 35 years of innovative and brilliant high school teaching. One of Hal's "pet peeves" is students sleeping in class or even just putting their heads down on their desks during class.

So the visiting teacher was confused by the seeming laxity of the urban teacher. Until he asked about it. You see, the visiting teacher has a mostly suburban population and teaches mostly Advanced Placement courses. These urban students were much more likely to come from chaotic homes and neighborhoods. Some of them were homeless. Many could not sleep at night, sometimes as a self-protective strategy. So they were too sleep-deprived to function effectively in school. They simply needed some sleep. And their teacher knew that and accepted it. There was no point in punishing them for something they could not control.

Third, you need to be sensitive to the signals your students send. Some are blatant, such as a student who has her head down on the desk and is falling asleep. Some are noticeable just because they are out of character, such as the typically giggly or gregarious student who is sullen and short-tempered. Others, however, are less noticeable, manifested only by slightly more distractible or nervous behavior.

Good teachers both intentionally look for and reasonably accurately interpret such signals. Some teachers are naturally sensitive to these signals in students, but others have to work harder to spot the clues. Some teachers, for instance, greet every child at the classroom door, not only to make them feel welcome and set a positive tone for the class, but also to look for any signs that something is awry. Hal Urban, in his book *Lessons from the Classroom*, describes how he greeted every student in every one of his high school classes for over a third of a century. Many elementary school teachers have a "3H" sign on the door (standing for "hugs, handshake, or high five") and each student gets to choose one as the greeting from the teacher as he or she enters the class for the day. As one teacher at An Achievable Dream Academy in Newport News, Virginia, said, as she greets each of her students in the doorway each day, she likes to "look them in the eye" to see if anything is wrong. Her point was that it might seem small or it might seem large to the teacher, but if it matters to the child, it needs to be dealt with so that child can learn that day.

Fourth, you have to be willing and able to ask a student to explain such behavior. This often does not come easily, both for the teacher and for the student. We are frequently reluctant to "butt into" people's personal lives. We are also typically hesitant to give negative feedback to people about their behavior. Additionally, we are often afraid of being wrong about a personal assessment. So a bit of interpersonal courage, altruism, and sensitivity is needed to talk to students about whether there is a rat on their brains. And to find out what that rat looks like for that student.

> **Steps in Successful Rat Removal**
>
> 1. Acknowledge that kids have lives and bring them to school.
> 2. Don't vilify students for having rats in their lives (and on their brains), especially when it is not their fault.
> 3. Be sensitive and open to signals students send about their rats.
> 4. Be willing and able to ask students to explain their behavior.
> 5. Create structured ways to make space in the classroom for students to unload their rats from their brains.

It also requires a modicum of trust on the part of the student. Students may not be willing to let you into their lives about matters that worry them, especially if doing so might be construed as embarrassing, stigmatizing, or making one socially vulnerable. It takes time and hard work to build trust, an important concept that is a recurring theme throughout this book.

Most of this deals with the kinds of rats that students are reluctant to talk about. In such cases, teachers need to be caring and gentle and supportive...and confidential. But Chris's rat was a different sort of rat. Not a bubonic plague carrying vicious nuisance, but an exciting one; one he was eager to share with the teacher and the entire class (and probably anyone else who would be willing to listen). These kinds of rats require a very different strategy.

Check-In Meetings

We know that even kindergartners can learn to "hold it" in the biological sense (at least most of them, most of the time). Likewise, Chris can learn to "hold" the rat. If he knows that there will be a more appropriate time to get that rat off his brain, then he may be able to push it to the side of his brain for the moment and effectively attend to class. How do you do that?

The best way I know is to build into the life of your class a structured means for Chris to get the rat off his brain. The workshop I am asked most frequently to present to educators is an introduction to class meetings. Fortunately, I have been studying and teaching about various forms of class meetings for over 30 years. For a long time, I was interested in one special form of class meeting called moral dilemma discussions. These are teacher-facilitated class discussions of open-ended moral conflicts. More recently, I have diversified because (1) I have learned so many other uses of class meeting structures and skills and (2) educators have been asking for help with this strategy for diverse purposes.

> Class meetings are a powerful and robust strategy that can be used for many functions such as problem-solving, collaborative planning, decision-making, gauging the sense of the group, teaching the academic curriculum, and reflecting on lessons and other experiences.

Class meetings have a long history in education and one of the earliest and strongest proponents was William Glasser, especially in his book *Schools Without Failure* (for an updated "spin" on Glasser's approach, I recommend Jon Erwin's *The Classroom of Choice* which covers many of the themes in this book). Class meetings take many guises, but the gist is that this is a pedagogical and class management method in which teachers facilitate students, ideally sitting in a circle, having an open honest and respectful discussion. Class meetings are a powerful and robust strategy that can be used for many functions such as problem-solving, collaborative planning, decision-making, gauging the sense of the group, teaching the academic curriculum, and reflecting on lessons and other experiences. One specific type of class meeting, however, serves as an effective means of cortical rat removal. These are called "check-in meetings."

In a check-in meeting, students are afforded the opportunity to present their lives, including those aspects of their lives that they most explicitly bring with them to school. Some teachers like to have check-in meetings every day (either at the beginning of the day/class or at the end of the day/class). An excellent character education program, *The Responsive Classroom*, has at its foundation what they call "the morning meeting." Each class begins each morning with a four stage class meeting. The first stage is a group greeting activity. The second stage entails students sharing news with each other. This is followed by a group activity that builds relationships and connectedness. The final stage centers on a discussion about a daily message. The process is detailed in Roxann Kriete's book *The Morning Meeting Book*, which is supplemented with suggested stage four daily message topics in Rosalea Fisher's book *Morning Meeting Messages*.

Some teachers like to have class meetings to end every day. Eric Soskild, a fifth grade teacher, noticed that the last 15 minutes of each day were wasted as students were clock-watching and not paying attention and hence not learning. So he instituted a class meeting during those last 15 minutes of each school day. Students would pack up their belongings, get their coats, and be ready to literally walk out the door when the bell rang. Then they would have a 15-minute class meeting, ending at the bell. This became such sacred turf to the students that, if Eric encroached upon class meeting time with the curriculum, the students would protest and demand their treasured class meeting time. One could easily imagine Chris in Eric Soskild's class, putting aside his rat until the end of the day if he knew that was an opportunity to discuss it.

Other teachers like to have a check-in meeting Monday morning or Friday afternoon. Others do it as the need arises. It is easier to do this with greater frequency in the structure of an elementary school where the students are with the same teacher most of the day. In middle schools and high schools, it would eat up too much instructional time to have a check-in meeting in each class each day, so the once a week format is more practical. Many middle and high schools, however, have homerooms or advisories at the beginning of each day. Such structures are ideal for rat removal. Most schools also waste homeroom/advisory time or are searching desperately for productive ways to use the time. Problem solved! Just use homerooms for rodent removal.

A check-in meeting is actually one of the easiest forms of class meeting to do. All one needs to do is sit in a circle, and go around the circle to take turns sharing something about oneself. For a good description of check-in meetings I recommend the book *Ways We Want Our Class to Be* by the Developmental Studies Center (www.devstu.org). Tom Lickona's book, *Educating for Character*, also has a chapter on class meetings that is very helpful. The point of this chapter is not to teach you how to do a check-in meeting, so I will only offer a few examples and tips. It is also important to note that for younger children, controlling the amount of time each child speaks can be a challenge. Using rehearsed sentence starters such as "One thing I'd like to share is..." or rules such as using only one or two sentences may help with early childhood or primary grade classes.

Conditions for Effective Check-in Meetings

Here are a few tips: First, there is some preparatory work necessary for this to go well. You should explain to your students what a class meeting is and why you will be doing them. More importantly, you need to agree on some behavioral guidelines and to create a classroom climate of trust, support, acceptance, and openness. I recommend that guidelines are collaboratively generated. If you want to know how students want to be treated, ask them. They will generate a fine list of norms and guidelines and they will largely overlap with what you would have generated. When you rent a car, do you treat it as well as your own car? We tend to treat our own things better than we do others. When students make the rules, they take better care of them including adhering to them more faithfully.

> When students make the rules, they take better care of them including adhering to them more faithfully.

Creating a safe and caring classroom climate is a bit more complex, but is dealt with in more detail in Chapter 12. So I will simply say it is a matter of what you model in the way you behave, how you treat children, what you tolerate, and the degree to which you intentionally promote positive relationships among all the members of the classroom community. Simply getting to know about each other and having positive experiences working and playing with each other is one way of achieving this.

When students know each other in positive ways, when you and they know each other similarly, and when they feel safe in taking chances and making personal disclosures in the public sphere of the classroom, then they can effectively engage in check-in meetings. And of course, the more you do this, the more they both get used to it and see that it is safe.

Sit in a circle and take turns sharing. One fourth-grade teacher has the students go around the circle and indicate verbally how they are doing "physically and emotionally" on a scale from one to five. "I am a five on both." "I am a four physically and a three emotionally." And so on. I happened to be observing her class one day when one boy, Alan, said "I am a five physically but a one emotionally." Students immediately were concerned about their classmate Alan and asked why he was an emotional "one," and he said that his "auntie's dog had died" and he was especially fond of this dog as he never had a dog of his own. This check-in meeting quickly morphed into a problem-solving meeting as students tried to take care of Alan. One boy suggested "what if you tell us all about your auntie's dog and then one of us could pretend to be your auntie's dog and we could follow you around all day and that would make you feel better." A charming suggestion indeed. In this case the rat was a dog, and the students took on the job of dog removal because there was a structure in the class to find the rats...or dogs on kids' brains.

Some check-in meetings can last only a minute as you whip around the circle. Some teachers like to offer students the option to "pass" if they do not want to share.

There are lots of ways to vary check-in meetings, but the real point of this chapter is that we need means of rat removal and check-in meetings are one good way to get the rat off Chris's brain (although clearly such meetings have a wide range of beneficial effects beyond rat removal). Then Chris will be ready to learn and grow. And as you now know, you simply can't teach through a rat. And there is no point in banging your head against a rat.

The Golden, Tarnished and Invulnerable Children

I really can't blame teachers for wanting the best students. Can you? After all, life would be much easier and one's job much less stressful and difficult if all students in your class were self-controlled, intrinsically motivated to learn and be good, and socially and emotionally competent. So I don't blame teachers for gravitating toward such students when they appear in their classrooms, and we know from research that teachers do just that. And they hope for more such children every year.

The Golden Children

I call such children the *Golden Children*. It is as if they were dipped in a vat of molten gold. They shine and sparkle and glisten in the sun like a brightly polished Oscar statuette. These are children who come from healthy families, in fact from exemplary families. Their parents love them and understand how to raise good children. These parents set a good example for their children by modeling what they want their children to do and to be and to become. Such parents tell the truth, help others in need, care about the general welfare, resolve conflicts productively, admit their errors, and so on. These parents also understand children, child development, and child rearing, perhaps intuitively or perhaps through reading about and studying child development. And they understand and accept the responsibility and obligation that comes with the role of being a parent. And throughout their children's lives, they poured their hearts and souls into supporting the most positive development of their children possible.

So their children grow up to be smart and good. The Golden Children come into your classrooms and look you in the eye, smile at you, and greet you sincerely and enthusiastically because (1) they like you, school, and learning, and (2) they are self-confident and socially and emotionally competent beings who generally want to, like to, and know how to have healthy relationships, not only with other children but with adults like you as well. When we discussed classroom greetings in Chapter 2, I mentioned Hal Urban's routine of greeting his high school students at the door each class period. He reports, however, that he had to teach most of them how to greet someone appropriately because only a few did it correctly and enthusiastically the first day. Those were likely his Golden Children.

The Golden Children work hard at school and genuinely want to learn. In fact, they like learning. What teacher wouldn't want that? In fact, these children often stay after class to ask you enthusiastically about academic material and sincerely want to learn more than the curriculum provides. When peer conflicts arise they solve them constructively if they are party to the conflict, and spontaneously mediate if others are involved. They elicit positive responses from all with whom they interact. And everyone loves them.

So it is not surprising that teachers love them too, and that they pay extra attention to them and give them special leeway and privileges. They call on them first and choose them more often for special jobs and roles. They spend more time interacting with them than they do with other, less golden, children. For Golden Children are a joy to have in class. And who in their right mind wouldn't want more joy in their classroom (and life)?

But there is one thing everyone forgot to tell you about the Golden Children. One little thing about those children upon whom you routinely lavish a disproportionate amount of your attention. One tiny little fact that you missed somehow. They don't need you. That's right, you heard me correctly. *They don't need you.* The Golden Children are on a fast track to success and even if you are a lousy teacher you are not going to derail them. You will bounce off of them as they continue on their merry way to a successful life. They will weather your lousy teacher storm. They, after all, are already great kids and they have great families to back them up. They are simply oozing resiliency. They are going to do just fine, with or without your presence in their lives. The Search Institute has a wonderful model called *The*

40 Developmental Assets. It is a list of 40 internal and external assets that we want children to have in their lives. Most people have some but not all. The Golden Children are hitting on nearly all, if not all, cylinders. Those assets (often called protective or resiliency factors) allow one to survive life's slings and arrows. They include things like: family support, positive family communication, parent involvement in schooling, and adult role models. So, armed with all these resiliency factors, the Golden Children will continue to sparkle, unblemished by your mediocrity or even ineptitude as a teacher. You are therefore, in one sense, wasting your time (sadly a disproportionate amount of your time at that) on such children.

The Tarnished Children

But not all students are golden. Some, in fact, are far from golden, as I am sure you are already aware. I call those children the *Tarnished Children*. These children come from dysfunctional homes. Their parents are abusive and/or neglectful. They psychologically bully their children. They ignore them. They beat or even molest them. They model all you would not want a child to observe or become: promiscuity, dishonesty, substance use, criminality, cruelty, failure to be a productive member of society, failure to craft healthy relationships, etc. And they have no clue about how children function and develop, or how to effectively raise a child. Nor do they care. Their children are not their sacred trust and responsibility; rather they are seen as superfluous or even a detriment or burden. So their children are broken. Seriously broken. And woefully tarnished. Unlike the Golden Children, they don't shine at all.

The Tarnished Children are children who don't smile, never look anyone in the eye unless it is for a confrontation, are often dirty and disordered in appearance, and have few if any friends. They elicit conflict and rejection from others. They don't do their school work and are defiant. They dislike themselves and they dislike others. They disrupt the classroom and school engaging in a range of undesirable and prohibited behaviors. They don't believe they deserve kindness and they don't expect to receive it. Furthermore, they are chronically suspicious of it when it appears. They are the "frequent flyers" in the principal's office. These are the type of children who have an uncanny ability to find your buttons and push them until you devolve into the mean authoritarian teacher you swore you would never be. You suddenly find yourself screaming uncontrollably at a five- or 11- or 16-year-old child and don't know how you got to that place until it is too late, the dust has settled and you have made a mess of the situation. These are the children who make it a school year where you wish you didn't have to go to work each morning, just because that Tarnished Child is going to be there ready to make your day miserable once again.

So it is not surprising that you avoid the Tarnished Children. You pray they don't end up in your class, and if they do you try to marginalize them. You let them slide for not participating because it is easier than confronting them. You ignore their minor disruptive behaviors because it is expected, perhaps even inevitable. You run to your principal and complain that you have too many tarnished children, yet again, in your class, pointing out that Mrs. Smith in the room next to yours has none...and didn't last year either. You are happy when these children are absent because of sickness. You are a teacher, called to service to children, and are pleased and relieved when a child is sick and can't come to school. And still I fully understand why you feel this way. These kids can make your life miserable (in and out of school) and make you feel ineffective as a professional (or even to doubt your professionalism entirely).

> Those same children you marginalize and ignore (or worse), need you desperately.
> You can be the single factor that changes the entire trajectory of that child's life.

But, just as for the Golden Children, there is one little thing everyone forgot to tell you about the Tarnished Children. One minor detail everyone seems to have forgotten to mention. Those same children you marginalize and ignore (or worse), need you desperately. You can be the single factor that changes the entire trajectory of that child's life. You can be the person that saves them from the likely array of negative outcomes that result from such backgrounds. You can fundamentally alter the courses of their lives.

You can be the difference between a life of misery (for themselves and those they touch) and a productive fulfilling life. We know from lots of research that such children typically end up with a host of common negative life outcomes. They are more likely to fail at life's major endeavors: relationships, school, family, work. They are more likely to experience negative life outcomes like divorce, joblessness, homelessness, imprisonment. And they are more likely to die prematurely from violence, drugs, risk-taking, criminality, etc. You can be the single factor that protects them from the pitfalls that otherwise await them. You can literally save that child's life. For the Tarnished Children, you matter, in fact you matter immensely.

The Invulnerable Children

Research has shown us that children from backgrounds like the Tarnished Children are highly likely to be psychologically unhealthy, to be unhappy, to be dysfunctional, and to generally have a wide array of negative life outcomes. But research has also shown us that a small percentage of such children beat the odds. A small subset turns out just fine. It is as if they walk through the sewer that is their lives and come out smelling like roses, something of a miracle it seems. But researchers have studied such children, whom they have labeled the *Invulnerable Children*. They find that there are some common characteristics that these children share and that the rest of the Tarnished Children, who do not fare as well, do not share. One of them is a healthy relationship with a benevolent adult who takes an enduring, nurturing interest in the child.

It might be an uncle or aunt. It might be a neighbor. It might be a professional youth care worker such as a social worker or youth organization volunteer. It might be a coach or a member of the clergy. Or it might be an educator.

Perhaps I should repeat that. It might be an educator. Once when I introduced the topic of invulnerable children at an inner-city elementary school, a teacher raised his hand and quite sincerely and naively asked, "Could I be that person?" If I hadn't destroyed my knees playing sports, I would have fallen to my knees and begged him, "Yes, yes you can! *Please* be that person to a student."

For a Tarnished Child, a teacher's love and interest in them can make all the difference in the world. These children have not known such a relationship and typically don't believe they could ever be the object of an adult's unqualified and healthy love. They base their expectancies and interpretations on what they have already experienced. They have "mental models" of adults generalized from the adults that they have known in their lives, especially those closest to them; that is, the dysfunctional parents that inevitably and by definition populate and decimate the lives of Tarnished Children. After all, that is a central reason why they are tarnished to begin with.

> For a Tarnished Child, a teacher's love and interest in them can make all the difference in the world. These children have not known such a relationship and typically don't believe they could ever be the object of an adult's unqualified and healthy love. They base their expectancies and interpretations on what they have already experienced.

So, working from the assumption that you are like their parents, they often resist or even actively work to undermine your benevolent attention, misperceiving authentic love or care as false and feeling like it violates their personal sense of the fundamental laws of nature. To them it is a disturbance of the cosmic order they have come to know. So you may have to persist, and persist, and persist. And remember that such children can be quite unlovable and test your patience to its limits and beyond, so it likely won't be easy.

But also please remember what is at stake. A child. A child's life and future. And all the wondrous possibilities within that child.

I highly recommend that you read Marilyn Watson's wonderful book *Learning to Trust*, which chronicles the two-year journey of elementary school teacher Laura Ecken as she learns, under Watson's tutelage, how to love Tarnished Children and create an almost magical classroom from a bevy of very tarnished kids. Part of that is understanding how they make meaning of relationships and helping them discover that the world does not have to be like it has been so far.

In Watson's words:

> Even though most teachers care about their students, it can be a challenge to form caring relationships with students who are difficult...these children often find it hard to believe that their teachers really care about them, despite the evidence that they do.
>
> When teachers have a framework that allows them to believe that even their most disruptive and disrespectful students want, deep down in their hearts, to be liked and respected, it will be possible to engage all students as partners who need assurances that they are worthy of care, as well as guidance and support, in their struggle to become competent members of the classroom community. It's important to be patient. Creating a classroom in which students and teacher alike feel trusted and cared for takes time. But it is that atmosphere of mutual trust and care that will lead to a naturally well-managed and disciplined classroom.

Watson mentored Laura Ecken to follow three key principles in transforming her classroom in this way. The first was to intentionally nurture warm, caring and trusting relationships with each of her students. The second principle was to nurture the development of friendly relationships between the students. Such an emphasis on not only positive relationships but mastering and implementing intentional, effective strategies for doing so is a recurring theme in this book, in part because relationships are the molecules that comprise healthy, effective schools and classrooms and the foundation for character development. Watson's third principle was to re-conceptualize student misbehavior as not merely an impediment to learning, but as an opportunity to support student moral learning and character development.

So, when you look at students and find your eyes gravitating to the Golden Children, and find your stomach clinching as you encounter the Tarnished Children, remember who really needs you. And remember for whom you can make the biggest difference. You matter to all the students, but you potentially matter most of all to the Tarnished Children. You can leave the biggest legacy with them. You can make the biggest difference for them. The Golden Children don't need you; the Invulnerable Children will find their own way through and beyond the rubble of their lives; but the Tarnished Children can't live, sometimes literally, without you.

Super Models

Years ago Charles Barkley made the well-known (and sadly, prophetic) claim that "I am not a role model." It would be fine, he implied, to emulate his basketball skills, as he was validated for that in part by inclusion in the National Basketball Association's Hall of Fame. But that should not qualify him and particularly the rest of his character and life as worthy of emulation.

What he seemed to be claiming was that he did not want kids to choose him as their role model; that he chose not to be their role model; that kids *ought not* to view him as a role model. Well, the latter claim may be what he preferred. He didn't want kids to emulate him. Fair enough.

But he also seemed to be attempting to opt out of role-model status. Perhaps, he thought that by publicly declaring it so, it would be so. He seemed to imply that his public declaration "I am not a role model" would somehow deter children from viewing him as a role model, that there was some form of role model exemption available to him (and by implication to the rest of us as well).

Well, here is the news for Charles and the rest of us: *being a role model is not a personal choice!* Never was and never will be. Being a role model is not up to the person being admired. They have little or no say in the matter. You don't get to choose to be (or not to be) a role model. Rather, you become a role model because others look up to you, emulate you, and imitate you. It is thrust upon you. In other words, it is the fan's or disciple's choice, not the hero's choice. By virtue of his celebrity on and off the basketball court, and his prowess as an athlete and the sheer power of his "larger than life" personality, exacerbated by his powerful presence through appearances in the popular media, Charles Barkley was likely to be a role model. Kids would see him, see his talent as an athlete, hear his dynamic and often controversial messages in the media (including his role model proclamation), and decide to be like him. That is how he became a role model.

> Being a role model is not up to the person being admired. They have little or no say in the matter. You don't get to choose to be (or not to be) a role model.

There is no "off switch" to being available as a role model, certainly not one that is under the control of the person being emulated. Then, sadly, one New Year's Eve, Barkley was arrested for a set of behaviors that no sane adult would want a child to admire. If he had control of the role model switch, then no harm to children would have been done. But we don't control that switch. The kids do.

All Adults Are Role-Models

The same goes for teachers. Pretty much all male students hope that their teachers will be super models. Well, they all are! First of all, it is not news that adults' behaviors influence children's character development. Over 2000 years ago, Aristotle observed that "all adults involved with children either help or thwart children's growth and development, whether we like it, intend it or not." And as Theodore and Nancy Sizer suggest through the title of their book, *The Students Are Watching*. Always watching. And they miss very little.

In other words, every adult in a school who comes into contact with children impacts their character development, for better or for worse. You cannot *not* (double negative intended) be a character educator. Character education is an enterprise from which you cannot abstain. It is not a personal choice, just as being a role model is not a personal choice. There is no off switch to character education, and there is no Harry Potter cloak of invisibility for educators. Every day, for good or ill, students are seeing you, and that includes all of your blemishes and missteps, and you are always impacting their character development.

The Students *Are* Watching

There are a few self-delusions that teachers seem to relish about this issue. One of them is that, contrary to the Sizers' contention, the students frequently aren't watching. If you will pardon my strong language, I say... Poppycock!! Balderdash!! This is utter nonsense. And we all have the evidence to the contrary.

All students that have ever crossed your path have a fairly deep opinion about you. Some are accurate, some are not. But they all have them nonetheless. And they frequently have nicknames for you as well. Some are flattering, others are quite the opposite. Some are pretty clever and others pretty mean-spirited. Sometimes you know about them, and other times you don't.

There is often mythology about you, often with no discernible basis in fact. This mythology (e.g., the reason you favor female students is because your wife and daughter died in a car crash...when no such thing has ever happened to you) can be passed down from generation to generation. There are students who entertain each other by doing impressions of you. And some of them are very good. You should see them! And students chart your clothing and jewelry. Phil Vincent (author of *Restoring School Civility*) reports that students in one class charted his bizarre ties and to his astonishment announced to him the first time he repeated a tie. I have also heard of students charting earrings and purses of their teachers. Just check the backs of the notebooks where they keep the charts (or on their Facebook page nowadays most likely). They don't miss much.

I recall one of my middle school teachers who had a rather pronounced set of verbal habits, expressions like "do you see?" and "can you see it?" which she repeated many times during a class. We created a baseball game from these. A "do you see" was a strike, a "can you see it" was a double, etc. We sat in the back of the class playing this game and focusing only on her verbal habits and not learning a whit of algebra from her. I don't think she ever even suspected. Probably didn't even realize we noticed her repetitive expressions at all. Yet that was what dominated our experiences in her class.

Think of something a student has repeated to you or more likely to the entire class, from something their parent had said or done, something that you know the parent didn't realize the child heard or saw and certainly didn't want the child to repeat or report to others. "My mom thinks Supermart is a rip-off on rolling papers." "My dad says teachers are suckers for working for such low pay." I am sure you have heard plenty of these. Well, if they are hearing this stuff at home, when the adults around them don't realize it, why do you think they don't do likewise at school? They are noticing the same stuff about you and going home to report it to their parents. There is symmetry in the universe.

If that doesn't convince you, and if you are also a parent, think of something your child told you that his or her teacher said that you are sure the teacher didn't think was heard and certainly didn't want repeated to you. My son came home from elementary school one day and announced that "Mrs. Smith (his teacher) gets all her furniture for free because her husband works on a loading dock. What's a loading dock, Dad?" I am sure Mrs. Smith didn't want her students running home to their parents and quoting her on this matter; and likely she said it when she thought the students weren't listening. Mrs. Smith was laboring under the same self-delusion that most educators do; namely, that kids only notice what you want them to notice. Why on earth would that be true?

Teachers frequently talk to their peers in the hallway or parking lot, talk on the phone to family and friends, or converse with the principal on the intercom. They also think the students don't listen in and process these conversations. They think that if the students are doing quiet work at their desks (for example, a test or work sheet), that they aren't processing the teacher's conversations.

Wrong.

Teachers often also don't realize the other messages they send through their body language, facial expressions, and tone of voice. Kids notice how you feel about your principal or fellow teacher or custodian by the way you look at them, your tone of voice in speaking to or about them, or simply your mood and demeanor after they leave the room and you return to teaching your class.

One way to understand this better is to accept that students are an oppressed class. I know this is not pleasant for you to accept or even grapple with. But they are and they share much in common with other oppressed groups. They are relatively powerless in school, a theme that is expanded in Chapter 9 on the parallels of schools and prisons and in Chapter 10 on empowering student "voice." Like any oppressed class, they learn, out of self-preservation, to closely monitor those in power over them and become very sensitive to the moods, messages, and behavior patterns of teachers, bus drivers, playground supervisors, etc. If you can't control what happens to you, then you need to at least be able to predict what will happen to you before it does, and perhaps avoid the undesirable stuff by staying astutely out of its way. It is a survival strategy, sometimes literally. Children of abusive parents learn to read the signals to know when the parent is likely to strike or not. So to assume they aren't watching is naïve at best.

Diagnosing Your Teaching

One epiphany came to me after a few early childhood and elementary educators independently taught me that the best way to know what kind of teacher you are is to watch your students playing school. They would quietly observe such role play. If the students depicted the teacher as a mean threatening figure ("That was super super bad, so I am going to take away your shoes and put you in the closet with spiders!"), that is likely how they see you.

I was always reluctant to share this clever assessment strategy with middle or high school (or college) teachers as I didn't think it applied. After all, high school students are not frequently caught playing school; however, know that they do mimic you to entertain their friends. I was hesitant, that is, until some high school teachers told me that there is a parallel phenomenon with their adolescent students. When students do a class presentation, they often try to mimic the teacher's style assuming that will get them a higher grade, because it purportedly reflects what the teacher thinks is "good teaching." Those teachers use the students' class presentations as a window into how the students understand the teacher's style. Administrators need to recognize that this same process happens for them and their staff. For example, how you lead faculty meetings is what teachers think you think is good pedagogy. Ted and Nancy Sizer were right; the students *are* watching, watching, watching. And they never stop.

Called to Teach

A second self-delusion common to teachers is that teaching is just a job. I disagree. Teaching is not a job. Rather, teaching is a calling. It is no less a calling that the calling to religious life or the calling to military service. Like those callings, teaching is a calling to service to others. In the case of teaching, the service is to the learning and development of children. Most teachers understand at some level when they choose education as their profession that it is students that draw them to teach. They initially go into teaching because of children. They certainly are much less likely to choose their careers merely or even predominantly for the social prestige or lucrative financial benefits. But many teachers either never fully grasp how deeply teaching is a calling, or they lose their way eventually and start to think of their work as merely a job. This fact is the foundation for the teacher renewal movement, inspired in large part by the work of Parker Palmer in his book *The Courage to Teach*. Palmer rightly notes that many teachers lose their focus and veer off course of what originally brought them to teaching, and his reflections on this ultimately led to a network of resources, workshops, and writings to help teachers rediscover the purpose(s) that drew them to the profession of teaching.

> All teachers are role models. And all teachers need to embrace that as a very powerful tool in their calling to foster the development of their students. It needs to be strategically leveraged, not distortedly denied.

If you think of teaching as a job, then it is easy to find shortcuts, and to shortchange your students. It becomes easier to reach the decision that you are not paid enough to be a role model. It becomes attractive to believe and choose Charles Barkley's dictum that "I am not a role model." But it is a false belief and an impossible choice. All teachers are role models. And all teachers need to embrace that as a very powerful tool in their calling to foster the development of their students. It needs to be strategically leveraged, not distortedly denied.

When a teacher wants to foster, for example, respect in students, she must be respectful herself. As Tom Lickona has said in his book *Raising Good Children*, "Respect is a two-way street." In other words, teachers promote respect in students in part by being respectful of students, colleagues, administrators, support staff, parents, etc. When students are humiliated by teachers, they learn to be disrespectful. When students hear their teachers using put-downs about another teacher, they learn to be disrespectful. When students hear their teachers disrespecting a parent (perhaps even their parent!) who is being uncooperative in what is clearly in the child's best interests, they learn to be disrespectful. When the teacher is condescending to the custodian who has been neglectful of the physical needs of the classroom, the students learn to be disrespectful.

Teachers Can Be Bullies Too

One of the very real but little-discussed plagues in education is bullying by adults. Students quickly find out which teachers (or other adult staff) bully children; and, if they are shrewd enough, try to stay out of their path and wrath. The teachers at Fox Senior High School (in the Fox School District in Arnold Missouri, a National District of Character[1]) discovered information about the ways that teachers can be bullies. The Fox High staff was so moved by the concept of teachers as bullies and the list of ways that teachers often act, frequently unknowingly, as bullies that they created a video they called "The List" in which teachers from the school simply reflected on ways they had bullied students without realizing it and how moved they were to come to the realization of how they needed to stop and become better role models.

> **Behaviors of teachers who bully:**
> - Use sarcasm to turn disruptions into confrontations
> - Compare children to one another, rather than seeing all students as unique.
> - Punish students for being unsuccessful, rather than helping all students feel successful.
> - Humiliate students, instead of educating them.
> - Let students know who's boss, rather than that they care.
> - Are judgmental, rather than judicious
> - Are reactive and blame students for the lack of order in their classrooms, rather than being proactive and creating classroom environments that foster good behavior.

1. Throughout this book many exemplary schools and districts are mentioned. One index of excellence is recognition by the Character Education Partnership as a National School of Character or a National District of Character. Many states also have State Schools of Character programs. For more details go to the CEP website: www.character.org.

I recall visiting a school to spend a day training the entire staff. It was a relatively small elementary school. The principal picked me up at my hotel and on the way to the school tried to quickly fill me in on the nature of the school. He was in his first year as principal and was learning the culture himself. As part of his orientation speech to me, he pointed out that there was one teacher to look out for. He didn't identify her as he said she would be apparent quickly. All he told me is that she likes to confront others, mostly her peers but including invited speakers, and publicly humiliate them. That was certainly a provocative and interesting revelation, but I was so caught up in the workshop I was about to present, that I quickly forgot about his warning.

Near the end of the morning portion of my workshop, one teacher described a behavior management strategy that she (and other teachers in the school) frequently used. I did not consider it an optimal practice and thought it pretty inconsistent with what I was trying to present as quality character education, so I pointed out some of its weaknesses. The teacher defended the practice. I countered the defense and offered alternative strategies that I thought would be more consistent with the perspective of effective character education. This back-and-forth continued a few more rounds and quickly ratcheted up a few notches, but I knew I had research and developmental theory behind me so I held my ground. Suddenly the teacher burst into tears and rushed out of the room.

At this point I felt like the misguided cross-bred offspring of an ogre and a jerk. I had let the debate go too far and consequently had intellectually bullied the teacher into tears. I wanted to stop the workshop and track her down and humbly apologize. But I had a room full of educators and lunch was about 30 minutes away. So I decided to continue (with half of my mind and much of my heart focused on the crying teacher) and planned to seek her out at the lunch break. As soon as it was time for lunch, I bolted from the room, both to escape my shame but more so to find the teacher and try to make amends. I searched the school, but I couldn't find her. So I returned to the group and grabbed some lunch and sat with a table of the staff, fully expecting the topic of conversation to be the rather startling events of my debate debacle. Not a peep. No one was discussing it. They were happily chattering about less significant but decidedly more benign matters. I blurted out, largely to reduce some of my painful guilt, how sorry I was to have caused such an unprofessional scene. No one took the bait. In fact, they seemed utterly disinterested in what was so agonizing and salient to me. To say I was confused, even flabbergasted, was an understatement.

After lunch, I continued the workshop, and the formerly crying teacher rejoined us, apparently in complete control of her emotions and quietly and uneventfully participated in the rest of the day. The workshop was going great and everyone seemed in good spirits. Except for me, of course. I became even more confused. At the end of the day, I sought her out and apologized and all seemed fine. Then I queried the principal because I was unable to understand this entire dynamic. He informed me that (1) this was the bully teacher he had alerted me about and (2) the rest of the staff were thrilled that someone had finally backed her down. I was, in a perverse sense, a hero to them for what I had done. I don't see it that way, but I understand their perspective. Apparently, this teacher had systematically and publicly humiliated each of the other staff over the years, many to the point of tears, and regularly took on presenters and tried to humiliate them as well, and had been spectacularly successful at it until this point.

The staff was all waiting with trepidation for her to do the same to me. They were thrilled and surprised when she failed.

Now, I am recounting this story because of how extreme and startling something is to me. And it is not the interaction I had with the teacher.

> We know from strong psychological research that children learn more from what we do than from what we say; and that they learn best when there is consistency between what we say and do.

Sadly, that is something I have experienced before when my zeal triggers my lack of tact. Nor is it the reaction of the rest of the staff. Rather what is most startling to me in this story is the fact that an adult school culture could even exist like this. I remain stunned that an adult professional community in a school could tolerate such a mean-spirited and aggressive colleague as they had done apparently for years. There is no place in a school for an adult like this. I don't care what her pedagogical skills are; she is poison for children's character. She will hurt some of them and model antisocial behavior for all of them. Her character is antithetical to being a character educator, and since, as we have already established, all educators are character educators, she has no place teaching children.

Actions Speak Louder Than Words

Another part of the role model self-delusion is the belief that kids learn from what we say and not from what we do. A teacher (or an entire school, for that matter) that verbally promotes respect (with signage, and inspirational quotes, and verbal exhortations) but acts disrespectfully, will not promote respect. We know from strong psychological research that children learn more from what we do than from what we say; and that they learn best when there is consistency between what we say and do. To quote Tom Lickona again "Practice what you preach, but don't forget to preach what you practice." It is the combination of behavior and rhetoric that is most influential of children's development, but behavior always trumps rhetoric.

> ### Common Delusions of Educators
> 1. Students only see and hear what we want them to see and hear.
> 2. Teaching is just a job.
> 3. All bullies are students.
> 4. Kids learn from what we say and not from what we do.
> 5. Teachers have little power to impact kids' character and development.

One wise but anonymous quote about modeling is, "The most powerful tool you have to influence the character of your students is your character." Mahatma Gandhi once urged us all "to be the change you want to see in the world." I implore you to be the character you want to see in your students.

Don't just aspire to be a model teacher. Aspire to be a model. A super model. Period.

Chapter 5

Why Don't We Do It in the Home?

I truly love teachers. Really I do. I hope that fact, despite my sometimes gruff tone, is evident from this book, which I wrote in order to help teachers help kids. The stories and ideas come from countless workshops I have done for teachers, most of them for free. (I am not trying to pat myself on the back here: I just want you to know that I'm not in it for the money. If you are like most teachers, neither are you.) I am fortunate that my job requires me to have one foot in the university and one in the community serving youth. I fulfill that in part by helping educators to help kids become the best people possible. And that in turn will help make the world a better place. Teachers are critical to that project. That's right; teachers are keys to saving the world. Very significant keys, in fact.

Unfortunately, what I have found over time is that all too many teachers, despite genuinely caring about kids and wanting to help them learn and grow, get stuck on the "how." Many teachers don't seem to grasp what will actually achieve the goal of fostering kids' character development and academic achievement. Chapter 11 includes data from a national study by the Character Education Partnership demonstrating that many educators already involved in character education know what effective practice is, but still don't do it. Many educators, however, don't even seem to know what works in building character.

Here is a little thought experiment I like to use with educators. First, I ask them how many of them are parents. Typically, most of them are. Then I ask them how many of them have a dream that someday their child will become a criminal and spend his or her life mostly in prison. When none do, I announce that I will assume they want their kids to develop good character. With that established, I ask the following set of questions:

1. How many of you begin each day in your home with a pithy quote about character, preferably delivered in a disembodied voice through a speaker in the ceiling of the kitchen?

2. How many of you have posters around your house, each with just a single word saying "Respect," "Responsibility," "Caring," "Honesty," etc.?

3. How many of you have renamed the spaces in your house, ideally with cute street signs, "Karing Kitchen," "Benevolence Bathroom," or "Happiness Hallway"?

4. How many of you walk around with little slips of paper in your pocket, and when your child does something good you give him or her one of them? At the end of the week, if they have five slips they can cash it in for an extra dessert.

5. How many of you convene your family once a week or once a month to announce which member of the family had the best character that week or month?

I may get one or two people who admit to items one, two or four, but usually not, and I never get any reporting that they do items three or five. That is when I lean forward and glare at the audience, who have said they don't do these things with their own children, and ask them, "If that stuff is so darn powerful, why don't you do it for your own children?" At that point, most of them get it. If I wait a few moments even more light bulbs go off. The uncomfortable giggles that ripple through the audience are quite telling.

I have found time and again that educators rush headlong toward these types of implementation strategies apparently without reflecting upon their actual value in achieving the goal of fostering student character development. Yet, paradoxically, at home they seem to intuitively understand that character comes from love, relationships, role-modeling, high expectations, thoughtful egalitarian discourse, etc. (all of which we listed in Chapter 8 on teachers as surrogate parents as the Fab Five of parenting for character). In the family and school contexts, teachers have the same good intentions of fostering character development, yet the methods are wildly disparate. What gives?

I honestly don't know, but I have my theories.

Why We Do What Doesn't Work

THEORY #1. Schools and colleges of education are failing our future teachers. This is happening in multiple ways, but two of the main ones are the following. First, we are not adequately teaching the research and theory behind promoting positive youth development. Our pre-service classes don't adequately address attachment theory, developmental discipline, socio-moral development, social emotional learning, etc. Second, our professors do not model the practices that they should want their students to implement eventually in the classroom. So our pre-service students, our future teachers, are not adequately prepared to understand and effectively implement the pedagogical strategies that actually foster student character development.

THEORY #2. When college students get out into the schools as part of their pre-service training, they are not seeing enough best practices from master teachers. They often, for all sorts of organizational and bureaucratic reasons, are placed in mediocre schools and mediocre classrooms. So they see rewards and posters and street signs and hear pithy but ephemeral morning announcements about various virtues. And they learn to do likewise.

THEORY #3. There is a saying that "you are what you eat." And we who have children all know that we become the kind of parents we had, often in ways we do not want to be. Well the same goes for teachers. By the time one gets one's teaching license, one has had between five and seven years of elementary school, and typically another seven years of middle, junior high, and/or senior high school. Oh, and of course there are at least four years of college, often more. In the U.S. system that comes to approximately 100 teachers during all those years in school. That is a lot of socialization and a lot of modeling about what a teacher is and does. We become our teachers, just as we become our parents. Unfortunately, students are often not aware of some of the subtler moves a teacher makes, so even if they have a teacher who does "get it," they will be more likely to notice the high glitz, low impact strategies that those and other teachers use, such as rewards, announcements, posters, etc.

THEORY #4. The effects of the long-term effective strategies, almost by definition, take a long time to see. One study of a comprehensive school reform model showed that there were immediate effects on student behavior and attitudes but that the eventual gains in academic achievement were only apparent many years later. On the other hand, the effects of high glitz, low impact strategies (like public humiliation or material rewards) are often immediate (albeit short-lived or even back-firing). So the ineffective strategies are more likely to be self-reinforcing than are the effective strategies, because what we notice most are the immediate gains, even if they are ephemeral and eventually disappear or even reverse course.

I have one more theory, but I will save that for the next chapter that focuses more specifically on the practice of using extrinsic motivators to foster, among other outcomes, character development.

The cost of using ineffective methods is very high. At stake are the futures of our youth and ultimately the future of our society.

Now, I don't really know which of these theories holds water, if any. What I do know is that many of the teachers I have worked with often cling to, sometimes ferociously, their favored but ineffective teaching strategies. They tend to resist encouragements to get them to change their ways, frequently and fervently mustering lengthy impassioned defenses of their practices. For example, the mere suggestion of not rewarding kids for good behavior (to be addressed in more detail in the next chapter) or stopping the monthly character assemblies where a few kids are trotted across the stage for having good character sometime during the past month, often elicits assorted defense mechanisms.

Even when educators do admit that a change would be in order, they seem to feel it would be impossible to wean the kids off the assemblies and/or rewards. One elementary school principal sincerely pleaded with me, "But how can we stop??!" My answer, delivered poker-faced, was that, "It is very complicated, so pay close attention. The way to stop is to... *just not do it anymore!*"

Interestingly, the assumption seems to be that the kids will rebel or go through some painful and scarring withdrawal process. However, what those who have courageously ventured forth and risked abandoning a formerly prized assembly ritual or venerated reward program have told me is that the kids never even asked about it. They either didn't even notice it was gone or didn't care.

As educators, we tend to greatly overestimate kids' attachment to "how things have been." In truth, they have a marvelous ability to adapt to change.

Where Does *Your* Character Come From?

Here is another way to think about what impacts character development. Take a moment to reflect on yourself. Not your teaching practices, but your character. Think of someone who knows you very well, for example, a close relative or dear friend. Pick someone who really understands you deeply and who also really likes you.

Then imagine someone who doesn't know you asking this person to describe you. Perhaps they will be meeting you soon and are curious what you are like. Now imagine what the close friend would say. Better yet, what would you hope they would say? What personal strength or character virtue would you hope they noticed and would choose to highlight in their preview of your character?

> I will bet you didn't become deeply and consistently caring because you won a monthly award for caring in third grade.

Now spend a moment pondering that strength. Perhaps it is your honesty, or that you are a very caring person, or perhaps it is your generosity of spirit and resources.

Whatever it is, now I want you to ponder just one more thing: Where did that character trait come from? Why are you like that, perhaps more so than most people? What are its roots, it sources?

Having done this exercise with educators many times, I am not merely guessing when I say that I will bet you didn't become deeply and consistently caring because you won a monthly award for caring in third grade. And you are likely not a generous person because of a poster you saw on a school wall. And you are probably not consistently honest because of a quote your high school principal read over the PA system at school one morning. And your abiding respect for all people is unlikely to have been generated by a sparkly pencil you received for being momentarily and moderately respectful once in seventh grade.

Rather your distinguishing character strength almost surely came from the way significant adults (most commonly, your parents but sometimes others) treated you and the behavior they modeled in their interactions with others. This is where the rubber hits the road. Loving relationships and setting a good example are two of the active ingredients in the formation of character, and, as will be noted in our Fab Five discussion in Chapter 8, these positive parenting behaviors are the same ones that "work" in schools and classrooms.

Yet we educators spend our own hard earned cash on poster after poster. On puppets, and trinkets, and bracelets, and sparkly pencils with character words on them. It is as if we think those posters give off some sort of character rays. Kids walk past them and are irradiated with "respect rays" which permeate their very moral souls in a deeply transformational process.

If you really want to be depressed, take the kids out of sight of the posters in your hallways or classrooms and ask them to tell you what is on the walls. They don't know. They don't even notice them. So unless the posters truly emit character radiation, they are probably not accomplishing anything. For me, posters and quotes are like highlighter pens. They lend saliency to something that already exists independently. If your school is a school of respect, then a respect quote or poster may make it more salient; that is, the kids will notice it more. But if your school is not already a school where respect exists, then putting up a poster proclaiming it is like highlighting a blank page. Or worse, particularly for adolescents, it breeds cynicism. And adolescents don't need any help being cynical; they are quite good at it already.

In Chapter 13, I introduce Charles Elbot and David Fulton's notion of a school touchstone. The reason a touchstone can work is because there is deeper meaning behind it and because it should be representative of the true nature of how people act and most importantly treat each other. Simply putting up a word, perhaps with a definition, without it being deeply understood and connected to the authentic norms and behaviors of the members of the school, or classroom, community can breed such cynicism.

So be a pioneer. Give it a shot. Try intentionally using, as consistently as possible, the effective practices—those that actually do foster good character. And stop wasting precious time and resources on those high-glitz, ineffective practices that you don't use with your own children.

Leaving Your Ex(trinsics)

There is an epidemic in education. It spreads from classroom to classroom like wildfire and it seems to infect teachers at an alarming rate. Kids are the ultimate victims, and teachers are the carriers who bring this infection into classrooms and pass it on to students. Some parents seem to catch it as well, most likely from their kids but perhaps from their interactions with their kids' teachers at open school nights and parent-teacher orientations.

The disease is an addiction; to the use of rewards and extrinsic motivators. I think we need to open a new organization called Extrinsics Anonymous. We need to get teachers to find a way to beat this habit and leave their ex(trinsics).

Just as I grappled more generically in the last chapter with why teachers use high-glitz, low-impact strategies so widely, I have grappled even more deeply with why they seem especially attracted to extrinsic incentives. This practice deserves special attention for several reasons: (1) it is so common; this may be the most frequent faux pas committed by teachers; (2) it is so intractable; teachers seem deeply resistant to even considering that using rewards and recognition may not be a good idea; and (3) whereas the other ill-advised strategies I discussed in the last chapter are ill-advised because they are ineffective (essentially a waste of time and resources), this one is not benign. It is, in fact, malignant.

It is almost like teachers are reward zombies staggering around schools in a pedagogical haze muttering, "I must give rewards. I must give rewards. I must stick bright and shiny things to students' clothing and papers. Sparkles are good."

In the last chapter I offered five theories about why teachers tend to gravitate toward and hang on to ineffective strategies. I also said I have yet a sixth theory and I would save it for this chapter. So here it is. During a teacher's education, there is a short half hour period that they can't recall. A total blank spot for which they cannot remember what happened. Think back; isn't there a short span of time during your pre-service education that you can't remember? See! My theory is that a nefarious educo-medical team sedated you and did some sort of secret advanced genetic engineering to make you and all other prospective teachers biologically disposed to give children rewards as motivators for good behavior. And to march them across a stage in front of a large audience to proclaim them momentary moral exemplars (or merely kids who came to school every day...or almost every day).

Somewhere in a secret laboratory they have been cross-breeding game show hosts, Ed McMahon's frozen DNA, Olympic organizing officials, and state lottery directors to create a pure strain of humans who feel utterly compelled to give things to others, most commonly for their behavior. They have then isolated the specific dominant genes and extracted them to inject into pre-service teachers during this sedated half-hour blank period. Okay, so this seems a bit far-fetched. Got a better theory? Because if this plot is not true, then I just don't get it. Why the heck are so many teachers obsessed with rewarding and recognizing kids and seemingly compelled to do so?

Why Rewarding Kids is So Seductive

Well a few possible, and more reasonable, answers to this question are:

1. **It's easy. Nothing could be simpler than giving kids candy, stickers, or coupons for doing the right thing.**

2. **It can appear to work—in the short run. Kids like getting rewards, and will perform the necessary behaviors to get them, at least for a while.**

3. **Behaviorist psychology, which nearly every teacher was exposed to in one or another college course, teaches that people, like pigeons and rats, will repeat actions for which they are "reinforced" (rewarded).**

4. **Discipline programs—such as Lee Canter's "assertive discipline" (beginning in the 1970s) and PBIS (popular more recently as a schoolwide system that uses "positive rein-**

forcers")—have been aggressively promoted and in many cases have reduced the frequency of behavior problems (even if, as I will argue, they don't necessarily foster the kind of character that operates when adults aren't looking or when there's no reward for doing the right thing).

5. Tangible rewards seem to reduce bad behavior and increase rule-following with particularly challenging kids—the chronic behavior problems—who don't seem to respond readily to "reasoning," punishment, and other methods.

So there is lots of blame to go around for the popularity of this particular approach to character education. But let me explain why I regard reliance on extrinsic motivators as the *worst* ineffective character education practice used by educators. Numero Uno. The Big Kahuna. Let me begin by taking you on a brief tour of my professional development.

Models of Human Development

I was trained as a developmental psychologist. One of the first things I learned was a set of core theories dominating the conceptual landscape of developmental psychology. I remember Professor Willis Overton's undergraduate class in developmental psychology at the State University of New York at Buffalo about 40 years ago. This was clearly the most challenging undergraduate course I took. (As I mentioned earlier, this class is why I went on to get a masters degree and then a Ph.D. in developmental psychology).

Overton was in the midst of writing an important theoretical paper with Professor Hayne Reese at the time, a chapter about what they called "models of man." They highlighted three dominant models of basic human nature in general and psychological development in particular: mechanistic, organismic, and psychoanalytic. I continued to use that model through graduate school and then as I taught developmental psychology for a quarter of a century. It really helped frame things.

For our purposes here, it is the first model that matters most. The mechanistic model comes out of behaviorism and assumes that humans are essentially inert, reacting only when the world around them acts upon them. They are shaped by their environments and are basically neutral, blank slates to be written on, as the philosopher John Locke opined in the 17th century. It is the environmental contingencies (rewards, punishments, etc. as consequences of behavior) that shape and reinforce (or extinguish) our behaviors and tendencies.

By contrast, the organismic model, to which both Overton and I dedicated most of our careers, assumes an active, thinking, partially self-directing human being who interprets his or her experiences and actively initiates and seeks them out.

Later, when I was done with my doctoral studies, I had the great fortune to spend two years working with Professor Lawrence Kohlberg at his Center for Moral Development and Education in the Harvard University Graduate School of Education. It was an exciting, formative time at the Center, and we were doing cutting edge work, some of which is presented in Chapter 9 "Sentenced to School."

How Rewards Can Backfire

I recall early in my time at Kohlberg's Center when Carol Gilligan, one of the leading faculty at Kohlberg's Center, was scheduled to speak to parents at a local elementary school about disciplining children. She had a scheduling conflict and asked me to fill in for her. I was relatively new at this and had not done public speaking before, so I spent a good amount of time preparing for the talk.

In doing so, I began to read about parenting practices in particular, and reward and punishment in general. What I discovered is that harsh physical punishment is a very ineffective means of controlling behavior. It tends to have many negative side effects, not the least of which are (1) hurting the relationship between the punisher and the recipient of the punishment and (2) often actually increasing the undesirable behavior that is being punished, and in cases of harsh punishment for violent behavior, even being directly modeled by the parent in the act of punishment. For instance, parents who use severe or abusive punishment often have children who are more violent and engage in more misbehavior. It was rather challenging to get parents to buy this notion that harshly punishing their children was not going to serve the intended purpose of the punishment and would likely undermine their relationship with their children.

It is worth noting that there remains a controversy over the use of moderate or mild physical punishment. I would rather err on the side of caution and not use such punishment at all. It still models striking another person when one is angry or frustrated with them, a message that can easily be misunderstood and misapplied by children.

> The single best treatment of this is Alfie Kohn's book *Punished by Rewards*. In a lengthy analysis, Kohn repeatedly and very convincingly makes the point that the reliance on extrinsic motivators runs a great risk of being counterproductive to student learning and development.

Many years later, as I began more consistently working in schools and with educators, I discovered more and more that (1) teachers rely heavily on rewards and punishments and (2) others were taking note of this. The single best treatment of this is Alfie Kohn's book *Punished by Rewards*. In a lengthy analysis, Kohn repeatedly and very convincingly makes the point that the reliance on extrinsic motivators runs a great risk of being counterproductive to student learning and development. If you are willing to hear a very strong and persuasive argument about the danger of relying on rewards and recognition in schools, I highly recommend reading this book.

A bit later, when teaching about how people struggle to effectively maintain a course of health improving life changes such as diets, exercise, smoking cessation strategies, etc., I discovered research showing that rewards get in the way of what is already a difficult psychological struggle for most people attempting such a change in their behavior patterns. In fact, the research shows that when one is already successfully building a healthier life pattern (e.g., staying on an effective diet; exercising regularly; adhering to a challenging and complex medical regimen) and someone then gives them a reward for their efforts, they actually become less faithful about sticking to their healthier habits. It becomes harder for them to stay the course when they are being rewarded for it. This is called the "undermining effect." Extrinsic reward actually can serve to undermine or weaken intrinsic motivation. This might seem counterintuitive, but it seems to distract from the intended message of the reward. Furthermore, it allows one to psychologically believe that the behavior was done for the reward and not because the behavior was worth it on its own merits.

Another epiphany for me concerning the potentially harmful effects of rewards and other forms of extrinsic motivation came when I was doing a workshop with the staff of an urban elementary school in a Kansas City. It was the start of the school year, and they chose to tell me a story about what had transpired the preceding year. Their goal had been to increase the service behavior of their poor urban students. And they reported significant success as the students engaged in more and more service as the year went by.

> Students had been receiving rewards for their service activities. They did more and more service as the year went on, but they apparently had done so simply or mainly to get the rewards for service activities. As a result, they had never really internalized the value of service.

At the end of the year the custodian announced his retirement. He had been at the school for decades and apparently was the most beloved character in the school (it is not uncommon for a loving, charismatic support staff member to have such a status in a school). So the teachers realized they had the opportunity for a "capstone" event. They asked the students to organize a surprise retirement party for the soon-retiring custodian as their culminating act of service for the year. The staff obviously had high expectations for this serendipitous opportunity to put the icing on a seemingly very successful year of promoting altruism and service as character traits in their students.

They were understandably flabbergasted and confused when the students completely dropped the ball on this endeavor, one that for all apparent purposes should have been intrinsically attractive to them to serve someone they loved and admired. Of all the service activities they engaged in all year, this should have been the one they cared most deeply about and committed most fully to.

When I asked them if they had ever figured out what went awry in this situation, they responded affirmatively. It seems that over the course of the school year, they had successfully increased student service by relying solely on extrinsic motivation. Students had been receiving rewards for their service activities. They did more and more service as the year went on, but they apparently had done so simply or mainly to get the rewards for service activities. As a result, they had never really internalized the value of service. If the staff had rewarded them for swearing or vandalism, they would have done that just as well. They had merely learned one of the sad, by-product lessons of extrinsic reward systems: go wherever the rewards are, and, conversely don't bother to go where there are no rewards. That is the lesson they learned about life and character. Because there was no reward attached to the retirement party, they found no motivation in organizing it.

You see, when we rely on extrinsic rewards for behavior we are really teaching two fundamental lessons. The first lesson is the intended one: do more of what you have been rewarded for or less of what you have been punished for.

However, the second unintended lesson is this: "We adults, the role models, the authority figures in your life, believe you should live your life by doing whatever gets you rewards." Period.

In the eyes of kids, we adults must appear to think extrinsic rewards are very important because we institutionalize them, rely heavily on them, and often make them nearly ubiquitous in the lives of children, particularly in school. But as we step back and think about this practice, it should become clear that (a) such rewards weaken kids' intrinsic motivation to do good, and (b) what brings rewards later in life in any given situation may not be doing the right thing but rather doing something that is immoral or illegal.

The business community is also starting to chime in on this one. They are complaining that their new young employees seem to expect to be rewarded and publicly recognized *just for doing their jobs*. Guess who they suspect is to be blamed for this? Schools. And I suspect they are at least partially right. Why, we even have institutionalized rewards and recognition for attendance! Aren't kids supposed to come to school? What message are we sending when we give special recognition to kids who come to school regularly? What's next, rewards for handing in homework, wearing shoes, or perhaps breathing?

One high school that had an epidemic of students simply not showing up for after-school detentions they had been assigned as punishment. So to solve this, they moved the detentions to lunchtime. The students still did not show up. So they created a prison guard escort system, where designated school members were waiting at the student's last class before lunch to escort them to detention. But they didn't have enough escorts. So their final brilliant plan was to offer a reward for showing up at detention without an escort. I am not making this up! Every student who showed up to detention without an escort was to get a free can of soda.

Now this is insane enough as it is, and it was done in an otherwise really good high school too, and by generally enlightened administrators and teachers. Rewarding kids for taking their punishment? C'mon!

But there was additional damage. Apparently the brand of soda given to the students was much better than what was available to the teachers in their lounge and the teachers were jealous.

We are breeding a new generation of kids who are well-trained to be reward and recognition torpedoes. They are out there like heat-seeking missiles finding the rewards and recognitions and aiming right for them. And there is a lot of collateral damage.

Educators and parents often fear the eventual or current anti-social youth, or adults, who may solicit their student/child to join, for example, an anti-social gang or some illegal scheme at work later in life. The enticement is likely to focus, at least in part, on the benefits of being in that. And those benefits are likely to be focused on two things: recognition and material reward. The former may be a pitch about everyone knowing who you are and respecting (read: fearing) you when you wear your colors and are associated with the gang. The latter may center on the money you will have from the gang's illegal activities such as selling drugs or stealing cars

That all seems pretty obvious. What you may not have considered, however, is the following. If your classroom or school tends to promote character by a focus, probably well-intentioned, on award assemblies and other forms of recognition and on reward systems, then you are likely teaching the same lessons as the elementary school above; namely, "We advocate that you focus on recognition and rewards and live your life accordingly." We structure our schools to teach this lesson and expect kids to adhere to it by striving to get recognition and earn the rewards that our schools so painstakingly create for them. So why should we be surprised when kids do precisely that: unwaveringly succumb to the attraction of rewards and recognitions. But you probably did not consider that you were grooming the kid to say yes to the gang solicitation. Just as Alfie Kohn says, our kids are being "punished" by our "rewards."

When Karen Smith first became principal of Mark Twain Elementary in Brentwood Missouri, she learned that they had monthly award/recognition assemblies. She suggested dropping them (which they did) because in her words, "The message we are sending is that every month there are a handful of kids who showed good character. Every day in this school hundreds of kids show good character."

I agree fully. In Chapter 18, the hidden messages we send, usually without realizing it, will be addressed more fully. This is clearly one of them. Furthermore, we need to ask ourselves what we are trying to accomplish with award assemblies.

I assume educators think that they are increasing character in the student body broadly. Think about it...did you become honest or caring because you saw another child recognized or rewarded for doing so? Then why do you think doing just that will work to promote the development of your students? More likely, most of the students in the auditorium (or cafetorinasium) are bored and not paying attention. And some are aghast: "SHE is the respect kid of the month!?!?!? She spit on me at recess and called Tommy a [racial slur]! This school is stupid. I hate it." Or frustrated: "I work hard every day to be as respectful as I can and no one ever notices. And she is a jerk and she gets the reward. I hate this school!"

Another excellent resource that I mention repeatedly in this book is Self-Determination Theory from Edward Deci and Richard Ryan at the University of Rochester (www.selfdeterminationtheory.org). They have amassed decades of excellent scientific research on intrinsic and extrinsic motivation, particularly as it relates to children and adolescents' behavior and learning. One of their major ideas is that classrooms that support student autonomy, which is addressed more fully in Chapter 10, have students with both better behavior and better academic achievement. Add to this sense of autonomy, the other two major motivators they identify (a personal sense of competence and a sense of connectedness to others) and you have a recipe for great schools and student character development and academic success.

Deci and Ryan also provide strong evidence of the counter-productive effects of a reliance on extrinsic motivation.

As still another example of this effect, let me tell you about a large urban/suburban high school with which I have worked. On my first visit, I met with a small group of students who were a cross-section of the diverse student population. At one point, one of them mentioned that they had a character reward program. It was not unusual. They had six character traits and they were color-coded. When students were "caught in the act" of manifesting one of the traits, they were rewarded with a color-coded plastic bracelet. If they received all six colored bracelets at the end of the year, they were entered into a drawing for a prize (reward).

Being against such extrinsic incentives for all the reasons already discussed, I thought this was a poor choice of a practice and was especially surprised that it would happen at a high school. The notion of cheesy colored plastic bracelets also seemed a bit immature to me for high school students. So I asked them about that. They said they loved them. And that, get ready for this one, students liked them so much that they stole them from each other! That's right. This was designed to promote character and instead it was promoting theft.

When I discussed this with the principal he told me that a black market had developed in the school just around acquiring these bracelets, presumably in order to be eligible for the prize drawing at the end of the year. To his credit, he put a stop to the entire practice.

And think about the theory of what children are like that is implied by all of these reward practices. If we start with a behaviorist orientation, we necessarily construe students as predominantly shaped by external forces out of their control. We, as allegedly enlightened adults, need to manipulate student's environments to control and shape them. Much like the way you train a pet dog. Yup. That is right. We implicitly see children like pet animals. To be shaped and trained without their participation and often without their knowledge. I, for one, refuse to think of children that way (as you will see in Chapter 12). And it grieves me that educators who love children and are called to a profession of service to children, even unknowingly, construe children in this way. I would not want my boss to think of me this way and then engineer my world accordingly. I doubt if you would either.

It Can Be Done!

Schools often ask what they should do instead of all this reward and recognition. First, simply stop giving them. As I noted earlier, educators seem to think doing so will somehow rupture the very fabric of the universe. In fact, students don't even notice it in most cases, and if they do they quickly forget about it. It is the educators who are obsessed with the seeming power of extrinsic motivation. What we want instead are kids who internalize core values and act because they authentically care about such values.

In Jennifer Dieken-Buchek's third grade classroom in Tillman Elementary School (Kirkwood, Missouri), the power of intrinsic motivation was demonstrated beautifully one day by an eight-year-old child. An administrator came into the room to announce that the class had won the "Silver Spoon" award for having the best cafeteria behavior that week. Along with it came an ice cream party from the cafeteria staff. Once the administrator had finished enthusiastically announcing this dairy bonanza, a student stood up and said, "Thank you, but we don't want the ice cream party." Dazed and confused, the administrator asked why the student would say such a thing. The reply was, "We should do it because it is the right thing to do, not because we get a party."

Jedi Teaching

I have been a science fiction aficionado ever since my best friend Fred Rosen got me to read Robert Heinlein's *Glory Road* in the fourth grade. I have never looked back. I read every book Heinlein wrote and then moved on to Clifford Simak and Isaac Asimov. Then for over a half a century continued to read as much good science fiction as I can find (and some that disappointingly was not as good). So I have read many versions of the notion of some kind of invisible force in the universe that a select few can tap into. And then they have amazing power. Perhaps the most salient version of this is the Star Wars notion of "the force" which Jedi warriors have learned to harness. We all watched as Master Yoda labored to get the young Luke Skywalker to find a way to connect to and harness the force as a way to do good in the universe and combat the evil forces of "the dark side" of the force.

Well, in a sense, teachers are Jedis too. They have the possibility of tapping into a powerful force in impacting students. And they are often fully oblivious to this power potential within them.

Unfortunately, many teachers seem to think that they are relatively powerless in the lives, development, and behavior of children. Certainly, it frequently feels as if you are powerless. There are often moments when children resist you, refuse to comply with your wishes or mandates, or seem to be impervious to your lessons, warnings, urgings, and exhortations. Don't let this fool you.

I cannot state this more eloquently than Goethe who wrote that

> **I have come to the frightening conclusion that I am the decisive element. It is my personal approach that creates the climate. It is my daily mood that makes the weather. I pos-**

sess a tremendous power to make a life miserable or joyous.
I can be a tool of torture, or an instrument of inspiration. I
can humiliate or humor, hurt or heal. In all situations, it is
my response that decides whether a crisis will be escalated
or de-escalated, and a person humanized or dehumanized.

Haim Ginott took this quote and applied it directly to his power as a teacher over the students in his classrooms. Hal Urban, author of *Life's Greatest Lessons* and *Lessons from the Classroom*, kept a laminated copy of the Ginott quote on his desk and read it every day for over three decades before the students arrived to remind him of how much power he had as a teacher to impact children's lives.

How to See the Power of Teachers

Think about a teacher who uplifted you, who inspired you, who motivated you, or who befriended you. Think of how you felt when she believed you could do more than you ever did, when she let you into some part of her private life by showing you her artwork or poetry, when she took time from her off-duty life to give you extra help or just to get to know you better. Then realize how you can still feel that warmth and glory of those moments all these years later. And for some of you, recognize how that teacher changed the course of your life; perhaps by inspiring you to become a teacher or just to go to college or even to see and reach for the possibilities in you.

Then think of a teacher you had who hurt you, even crushed your spirit. Perhaps she humiliated you in front of the class, or told you that you were not going to succeed in an assignment, in the course, or perhaps in life. Is there a teacher who devalued you because of your gender, your parents' lack of education, your race, your weight, or your appearance? Think about how you felt, how much it hurt. And then realize again how you can still feel the pain of this relationship and interaction so many years later; how it still hurts.

When I do this as an exercise with teachers in workshops (for a more complete description see Chapter 11), there inevitably is a story or two of public humiliation. And frequently those stories are decades old, even a half century or more. And they remain poignant after all those years. And it is not uncommon for a teacher to begin to weep in retelling something that happened in a five-second span 20, 30, 40, or more years ago. Something the perpetrator did not remember even an hour later.

That is awesome power, the same power you have over children every moment of every day. Re-read Goethe's quote. At a faculty meeting, ask people to share their stories of being uplifted or humiliated by a teacher when they were students. Share in pairs first, and then share your partner's story with the entire staff. Talk about how teachers shaped who you are today. Collect the key characteristics of the uplifting and demeaning teachers. Let this be your blueprint for the kind of teacher you want to be; the kind of role model you want to be.

> Reflect on the fact that all teachers leave their marks on children every day. Some of those marks are temporary, like the rub-on tattoos that children use. But some are indelible.

Perhaps, in fact hopefully, you have had that wonderful experience of a student coming back and telling you how important you were in that student's life. How the time spent in your classroom left an indelible mark of goodness on her. Spend time reflecting on those students and those amazing revelations that validated your calling to education.

Another way to demonstrate the power of an educator is to think about the times when you could tell which teacher a specific student had the previous year just from the student's behavior...and character. When you teach students who come from multiple "feeder" classes (for example if you teach fourth grade and there are four third grade classes, all of which feed your class), you have probably realized that students coming from one teacher tend to be very different than students coming from the other teachers...for better or for worse. Last year's teachers have an impact on the character and behavior of this year's students. Well, we all are someone's last year's teacher. That, too, is awesome power.

Reflect on the fact that all teachers leave their marks on children every day. Some of those marks are temporary, like the rub-on tattoos that children use. But some are indelible. Fortunately, some of those marks may be uplifting, inspiring, life-affirming, even life-saving marks. But others are painful and indelible scars, scars that throb with the memory of emotional suffering at the hands of an insensitive or even malicious teacher. And most of the times you will never even know that you left those marks. Rarely are you told how you have marked a child. But you do it every day. Every single day.

> **Meditations on Teacher Power**
> - Recall a teacher who inspired you or wounded you.
> - Read Chaim Ginott's quote (or Goethe's original version) every day.
> - Have a staff discussion of the ways teachers have impacted their lives, both positively and negatively.
> - Think about times when you could tell which teacher a student had the prior year by the student's character and behavior.
> - Meditate on the former students who have come back to thank you well after they have left your classroom.

Then perhaps you will be able to hold onto the realization that you are engaging in a sacred trust, a true calling to service to contribute to the precious lives that your students can live. And that you have awesome power to impact those lives in so many ways. Be a Jedi and embrace the force so you can have the most intentional and positive impact on students possible. When one is gifted with power, one should shepherd it responsibly. This goes for all Jedi teachers, too.

Chapter 8

Who's Your Daddy
(and Your Mommy)?

Let me say at the outset that, if you are adult working in a school, this chapter applies to what you do. I don't care if you are an early childhood educator working in a pre-school setting, a middle school special educator, a high school chemistry teacher, or even a college professor. Or support staff. This chapter still applies to you. I want you to know that so that you don't stop reading and skip to the next chapter or close the book after reading the next sentence.

All educators, whether they know it or not, and whether they want to be or not, are surrogate parents to their students. That's right; you are a parent figure to your students, whether you are teaching counting to 10 to four-year-olds or multiple regression to doctoral students. You have the influence of a parent in so many ways whether your students are not yet potty-trained or are 50-year-old returning college students, perhaps even older than you are.

This may sound bizarre, but it is nonetheless true. Let me explain. First, there is a hierarchical relationship between teacher and student. The teacher purveys learning and development; the student receives it. The teacher has authority; the student is subject to that authority. The teacher is expert; the student is novice. The student performs and the teacher evaluates the performance. And so on.

Now, I don't mean to suggest that this hierarchical relationship is absolute and inviolable. We can all think of times and ways that it flips. One very common example in the modern world is around technological issues. Very often students are more knowledgeable and proficient with technology, including educational technology, than are their teachers, and they consequently become the experts and helpful resources to their teachers in such matters. And with the world of information made so much more accessible to all, students will frequently have knowledge that surpasses that of the teacher in specific areas.

On the dark side, one of the most disheartening things I ever heard in a school came from a middle school student who said "Our teachers are afraid of the black kids." I was stunned and realized that this was as strong a condemnation of the health of a school as I could imagine. In that school, there was a small group of lower-class minority, mostly African-American, students who were a behavior problem, but were charismatic for the other, mostly white suburban students who followed them into the exciting world of youth misbehavior. The teachers were unable to manage this dynamic and had apparently lost the psychological power struggle with the key perpetrators. And worst of all, the students knew it.

> In a student-teacher relationship, the teacher has immense power and influence. And much of that comes from the surrogate parent-child nature of teacher-student relationships.

However, a situation like this is fortunately unusual, and in most cases the adult to child parent-like hierarchical relationship holds true. One place that it very frequently remains steady is in the emotional arena. Students often *feel* that their teacher is an authority and in charge (whether the students like it or resent it, or even try to deny it.).

The irony is that it is less likely to be felt reciprocally by teachers. All too often teachers feel out of control and educationally impotent. They think that students routinely disregard them, which of course they sometimes do. They think that they are powerless to produce student academic learning, and indeed there are real impediments here. They feel that they are utterly powerless to control student behavior. They seem to not be fully in touch with the degree with which students are impacted by them and the degree with which they influence student development and momentary emotional states. As we noted in the preceding chapter, they are wrong. Of course there are moments when they are ineffective. But it is foolish to generalize from these. In a student-teacher relationship, the teacher has immense power and influence. And much of that comes from the surrogate parent-child nature of teacher-student relationships.

This message is not surprising to those who teach younger students, especially pre-school and earlier elementary grades. Such teachers understand how young children look up to them and respond to their affirmations or castigations just as they would to their parents' similar behavior. They understand that effective behavior management is largely the same from a parent or a teacher. They understand that students emulate them. They understand how important their love is to students. They see daily evidence of how they, like parents, are objects of emotional attachment, sources of solace and security, to the young children for whom they also have parent-like responsibilities for not only their learning, but their socialization and nurturance. It is those who teach older children, adolescents, and even adults, who often don't accept the parent analogy I am presenting here.

But sometimes even the teachers of the little ones don't get this. I was recently teaching a workshop on class meetings to a group of K-12 educators. In doing so, I was promoting a pedagogy of empowerment (see Chapter 10) and suggesting that teachers allow students more say in decision-making, planning and problem-solving. After the workshop, two kindergarten teachers approached me and voiced their concern about giving their students all the control in the classroom through such class meetings. They were concerned that the students would reject the teacher's claims of authority and it would undermine the entire class dynamic. I was stunned. I simply told them that no matter how hard they might even try to give up their authority to their kindergarten students, they simply couldn't. It is impossible. They will almost always be experienced as adult authorities, as surrogate parents, by their five-year-old students no matter how much "voice" they give the kids in class meetings (or in any other way). It is simply in the nature of young children.

But this applies to teachers of older students as well. When I was working with Lawrence Kohlberg on his *Just Community Schools* project at Harvard University in the late 1970s, we tried as hard as one could in a public school to give students as much power, voice, and authority as possible. This project used direct democracy (one person, one vote) in small (about 100 students and four or five teachers) experimental high school units to build moral communities, which is described in more detail in Chapter 13. Try as we may, however, the "voice" of a teacher always seemed to carry more weight than that of a student. We were simply unable to get the students to fully hear teachers' voices as equivalent to their own. This didn't mean students don't disagree or dissent, but rather that they "hear" adults' voices with more authority than they hear the voices of their peers.

Remember, we are talking about 16- and 17-year-old adolescents here. The same ones who drive you crazy at home because they seem to think they should be peers to their parents. Ultimately, we had to resort to acknowledging this dynamic and leveraging the power of teacher "advocacy" because their voices did carry more weight. I have even seen the same dynamic throughout my career as a professor, with students, often much older than me deferring to me as a parent figure.

The "Fab Five": The Same for Parents and Teachers

Many years ago, John Grych, a child clinical psychologist at Marquette University, and I wrote an article demonstrating what research has shown us about the impact of parenting on children's character development. We targeted eight character aspects that we knew were fairly well researched: an orientation to social relationships; empathy; altruism; conscience; moral reasoning; self-control; compliance; self-esteem. Then we reviewed the research on the effects of parenting on each and identified what I call the "Fab Five"; that is, five parenting strategies that collectively promote the development of these aspects of character.

> **The Fab Five:**
> **Five Core Parenting Strategies for Promoting Character**
> 1. Nurturance: Care for and about the child
> 2. Demandingness: Setting and supporting high expectations for the child
> 3. Modeling: Being the character you want to see in children
> 4. Induction: Justifying praise or reprimand by focusing on the consequences of the child's behavior for someone else's feelings
> 5. Democratic Parenting: Empowering children's voices and autonomy

Interestingly, when a colleague read the paper he suggested we write a similar paper for educators. I was naively surprised. At this point in my career, I was largely working in developmental psychology and at best dabbling in applications to education. I didn't see the transfer from parenting to teaching. Fortunately, I heeded my colleague's sage advice and John Grych and I wrote a second paper making largely the same arguments for teachers. I felt relatively safe doing so as the journal that invited us to write the paper was targeted to early childhood educators. I don't think that back then I would have fully understood that the same advice applies to all educators. Now I know better.

As I noted in Chapter 4, all students study their teachers and frequently try to copy them, especially when thrust into a teaching role. Pre-schoolers do, adolescents do, and college students do. So I slowly began to recognize that being a surrogate parent is something that applies across the board for educators.

Some excellent research by Kathryn Wentzel further reinforced this revelation for me. She decided to see to what degree well-studied effective parenting strategies work when used by middle school teachers. The set of behaviors she selected were highly similar to the Fab Five that John Grych and I had already uncovered in our research. This is not surprising as a lot is known about effective parenting from a century's worth of research around the world. What she found was that (1) middle school teacher behavior can easily be coded as analogous to parenting behavior and (2) middle school teachers who use more of these tested and desirable parenting strategies have students who learn more and behave more positively.

This is not limited to pre- and neo-adolescent students in early childhood centers, elementary schools, and middle schools. Sadly many high school teachers believe just that; that is, that up until high school, it is fine to take a nurturing parental approach to teaching, but high school is where education becomes more serious and academic and a nurturing approach is no longer appropriate or functional. It is viewed at worst as having no place in "real" education and at best as a luxury that one cannot afford when one is preparing students for the worlds of work or higher education. Unfortunately, this is sadly misguided.

One large-scale study of high schools looked at the presence of two of the major factors in effective parenting: "structure and support." These parallel the first two of the Fab Five: demandingness and nurturance. And they represent the basic aspects of the most well-studied and successful form of parenting called "authoritative parenting" which itself has been linked to a broad range of positive developmental outcomes for the children of parents who use this type of parenting. Well, Anne Gregory and her colleagues at the University of Virginia found that high schools that score high on structure and support have students who engage in less bullying and victimization. So the finding that schools and teachers who use practices that are known to be effective for parents tend to promote better learning and more character in their students, from early childhood through high school.

> Anne Gregory and her colleagues at the University of Virginia found that high schools that score high on structure and support have students who engage in less bullying and victimization.

This is one of those findings that through hindsight seem so obvious, like inventing suitcases with wheels on them (I remain amazed that no one thought of that one sooner). Don't let that fool you. It may seem obvious in hindsight, but it is far from obvious from the other direction, and many if not most educators of adolescents still don't buy it. What a shame, as they lose because they are not using strategies that promote learning and development and their students lose for the same reasons.

In Loco Parentis

Another perspective on the teacher-parent analogy is that teachers actually have, although they often don't know it or have forgotten it, legal authority to function as surrogate parents. When a student steps into your school, you are *in loco parentis*. This Latin phrase, which means "in the place of a parent," refers to the fact that during the time that a student is in the custody of a school (and this includes the bus trip to and from the school, by the way), the school and representatives of the school (e.g., bus drivers, teachers, principals) have a legal responsibility to act as a parent in many ways. This means you have the authority and obligation to act in lieu of a parent should the circumstances arise. For example, if a child's health is in jeopardy, you are required to take responsibility to see that the child receives appropriate care.

In other words, the law says you are a surrogate parent. So if you don't want to take it from me or from solid educational and psychological research, take it from the law. Use the knowledge that you are a surrogate parent to leverage that relationship for the benefit of the student's academic learning and character development.

Summing Up: How to Be an Effective Surrogate Parent

So what should you do? Do as the successful teachers in Kathryn Wentzel's studies did. Use the Fab Five! A great resource on the Fab Five is a book edited by David Streight entitled *Parenting for Character: Five Experts, Five Practices* and is distributed by the Center for Spiritual and Ethical Education. It is five chapters by five authors, largely based on my work with John Grych, and I wrote the chapter on "democratic family practices." So here are some tips for you surrogate parents based on the Fab Five:

- **First, love kids.** Glory in them. One of my new theories of education is my "hoot theory." It goes like this: teach kids at the developmental level that you most get a hoot out of. If kindergartners tickle your fancy, teach them. If you find middle schoolers to be a hoot, teach them. Those of you who find middle schoolers to be a hoot, by the way, are a special breed and should be paid handsomely and locked in the building so you can never escape. And even more precious are those who naturally get a hoot out of the tarnished kids. Find what is fun and joyous about kids. Regale in each one's strengths and weaknesses. And let the love shine. Let the kids know how much you value being around them and knowing each one of them.

- **Set the bar high.** Demand a lot from them. This goes both for academic achievement and for behavior in general. Let them know what you expect (and therefore what you believe them capable of). But build support systems to help them get there. Scaffold for them. And monitor how they are doing. Give feedback, support, etc. to help them on their journeys to excellence. I highly recommend Ron Berger's book

An Ethic of Excellence as an example of this dynamic between teacher and student.

- **Use induction.** Give clear reasons for your evaluations of students (either praise or criticism) and focus those explanations on the consequences of the child's behavior for the feelings of others. Use this frequently as a means of getting kids to reflect on their successes and stumbles and to connect them to the effects of their behavior on others.

- **Model** what you want your students to do and be, just as I have discussed at length in Chapter 4. Be the character you want to see in your students. Tell the truth, act responsibly, respect others, be fair, etc.

- **Empower students' voices.** Create democratic structures in your classrooms and schools. Give students appropriate co-authorship of their educational experiences. Allow them the responsibility and opportunity to make choices and influence their classrooms and schools.

Taking the Fab Five to the Classroom

1. Love your students. Find what is fun and joyous about them and teach the age group that you find the most loveable.
2. Set the bar high for both academic achievement and behavior. But be clear and fair and then be sure to scaffold the competencies and resources they need to succeed.
3. Give clear reasons for your evaluations of students and be sure they understand them.
4. Model what you want your students to be and do.
5. Empower students' voices. Create democracy in your classrooms and schools.

Just as any good parent would.

Sentenced to School

Right after I earned my Ph.D. in developmental psychology in 1977, I went to work for two years at Harvard University's Graduate School of Education. I had been hired by Lawrence Kohlberg, a leading figure in both education and psychology, to work on his Just Community Schools project along with a stellar team of, among others, Clark Power, Ann Higgins, and Joe Reimer. The Just Community Schools concept was radical and had been percolating in Kohlberg's mind for quite some time. Building on Jean Piaget's pioneering work in children's development of thinking, Kohlberg had identified a series of stages of thinking about right and wrong that he claimed were sequential and universal; that is, everyone developed through those same stages regardless of whether they were American or Korean or Turkish or Namibian (at least the same stages for as far as the individual developed because people stopped at different stages and very few made it all the way to the highest, sixth, stage).

One of Kohlberg's interests was in how to maximize this developmental process; in other words, what could lead someone to develop faster and/or further, or even remediate delays, in their development through this sequence of moral reasoning stages? He tended to focus on education, on schools. He tried to blend a few experiences he had had with some theories he had studied and create an ideal school model for moral development. When he was asked to create a small experimental school within Cambridge Rindge and Latin High School in the early 1970s, he realized it was time to put up or shut up. Hence the Cluster School was born.

Cluster, and other schools like it (to learn more, see Clark Power, Ann Higgins, and Kohlberg's book *Lawrence Kohlberg's Approach to Moral Education*), were experiments in radical school democracy in small schools within larger high schools (the model has since been applied to other school settings; and even non-school settings, but more on that below). One person (teacher, student, etc.), one vote. The focus, as evidenced by the name, Just Community School, was on using democracy to promote justice and a community in the school setting. It was an exciting time and an exciting experiment, and it successfully stimulated moral development in the students that participated.

But that is not why I am telling you about the Just Community Schools. The reason, rather, is embedded in the other place that Kohlberg began experimenting with the model: the Niantic (Connecticut) Women's Prison. And, subsequently, in other prisons and other correctional settings.

Schools and Prisons

That's right; the Just Community model was initially implemented in high schools and prisons. You may wonder why Kohlberg chose such seemingly different types of institutions in which to apply his model. I know I did. At least until I started to look a bit closer and think a bit more deeply about this puzzling set of strange bedfellows: schools and prisons.

Well, the answer is that all is not what it seems to be. High schools may *seemingly* be different from prisons, but appearances can be misleading. In fact, high schools are alarmingly similar to prisons. Indeed, *all* schools are alarmingly similar to prisons. Now I know from lots of experience that educators do not like reading those last two sentences. Especially the elementary school folks who are aghast at this analogy. But indignation has never been a good measure of truth. So please bear with me as I try to make my case.

Let's take a closer look at the similarities of prisons and schools.

- Where else but prisons and schools are the "residents" told by authorities when to stand and when to sit?

- Where else are they told when to move and when not to move? And if told to move, told at what speed to move in particular places and at particular times?

- Where else are they told when to be silent and when to talk? And if allowed to talk, told at what volume to talk, and even which words to use and which not to use?

- Where else are they told what to wear and what not to wear? And often with a detailed manual or "dress code."

- Where else are they told when to eat, what to eat, how to eat, where to eat, how fast to eat, and when to stop eating?

- Where else are they told when to go to the toilet? And with whom to go to the toilet? (I have even seen schools where the doors are removed from bathroom stalls to have greater vigilance of students even when there!)

- Where else do we routinely have a weapons screening process at the entrances, with locked doors, metal detectors and an armed law enforcement presence?

- And, where else but schools and prisons are these same "residents" subject to sanctions, often severe sanctions, if they do not comply? And where else but schools and prisons do those who are subject to those rules and sanctions have little or, more likely, no say in the rules and sanctions? And where else but schools and prisons, do those who are subject to the rules and sanctions have little if any viable means of resisting, protesting, or appealing them? In fact, they have little or no say in almost anything meaningful that happens to them in those institutions.

That seems like an awful lot of parallels between schools and prisons and between the circumstances, the plight, of students and prisoners.

Schools and prisons are indeed alarmingly similar institutions. Students, like prisoners, are a markedly disempowered and even oppressed class. In fact, some schools are being criticized as being better at preparing students for a life in prison than for a life outside of it. Pedro Noguera, the Agnew Professor of Education at New York University, has written extensively about this issue. One of his core arguments is that schools are built to sort students, largely by the tracks they expect them to follow after school (for example, college or work or the military). But then schools treat students differently based on this, and this is not limited to what they teach them in each expected track. That alone is somewhat controversial.

What Noguera further argues is that schools with an overrepresentation of students expected to fail or even just struggle academically (for example, alternative schools for struggling students, vocational schools, inner city high schools):

Often operate more like prisons than schools. They are more likely to rely on guards, metal detectors, and surveillance cameras to monitor and control students, restrict access to bathrooms, and attempt to regiment behavior by adopting an assortment of rules and restrictions.[1]

There is a task force in St. Louis that focuses on preventing what they call the "school to prison pipeline." For so many urban high schools have turned into feeders to our prison system. The argument is that schools, particularly urban high schools, are doing a better job of preparing students for a life in prison than for college or work. And too many of our urban high schools are just like that. But it is not these extreme cases that I am concerned with. I am not just talking about embattled urban high schools; I am also talking about your friendly neighborhood suburban warm and fuzzy elementary school.

I know that this is not a thought that educators take to easily. When I present this concept in workshops, I see shock on the faces of the educators present. Sometimes I see anger and resistance and resentment. So I expect you may be thinking that I have gone too far. That I have forced an analogy. That I am engaging in sensationalist rhetoric.

But that is okay. After all, this book was designed to engineer epiphanies, and to create some cognitive conflict along the way. I know from experience that if I let you mull this over for a bit, some of you will start to have light bulbs go off over your heads. You will have an epiphany of sorts. This is even more likely if you take the radical step, as I have many times, of actually asking students to describe what it is like to be a student, and more importantly what their relation is to school and educators. Just ask the kids and you will suddenly see schools, indeed your school, differently than you did before. And that is precisely my goal in this chapter and throughout this book. Now most kids won't likely explicitly call their schools prisons (although it is not as rare as you think among adolescent students), but they will tell you how disempowered they are, and sometimes how trapped they feel.

Schools are inordinately hierarchical, authoritarian institutions. And they are embedded in larger hierarchical, authoritarian institutions, in fact in a long unidirectional tower of power. Starting with the federal govern-

---

1. Noguera, P.A. (2003). *Schools, Prisons, and Social Implications of Punishment: Rethinking Disciplinary Practices.* Theory into Practice, 42, 341-350. Quote is on page 345.

ment, power is directed downward, a point emphasized by Tony Wagner and Bob Kegan in their book *Change Leadership*. The federal government pushes down on the state boards of education which push down on the state superintendent who pushes down on the local school boards which push down on the district superintendents who in turn push down on the school principals who push down on the teachers who push down on the students who are the bottom of this pillar of pressure. If this were an organic process we would be turning our students into diamonds or emeralds, into precious gems. Instead we tend to be pulverizing and disempowering them. Of course you can identify exceptions to this, but I am interested in the larger pattern, not the exceptions here.

Students have little if any official power. And they know it. As I said, just ask them. Of course, you never hear their opinions on this because their voices tend to be stilled, uninvited, even suppressed; yet another symptom of this hierarchical structure, something addressed in the next chapter. And this affects how they feel about school as well as how they function at school. We know from educational research as well as parallel research in other spheres of life, that when people feel connected to an institution they perform better. When people feel shared ownership in an institution, they perform better. When they feel valued by an institution, they perform better. When they simply feel known in an institution, they perform better. Disempowerment marginalizes one, makes one feel disconnected, oppressed, de-valued, and unknown, essentially the core of Karl Marx's theory of alienation.

And if you don't believe me, simply ask some students. Especially middle and high school students who have the ability to deeply reflect on such issues, but later elementary grade students will tell you the same. Those stilled voices will come forth if invited in a way that feels safe and authentic. If you ask them, they will tell you that the school is unfair (not a just community), that they have no power and no one really cares what they think or feel. Furthermore, they will readily critique and de-construct the school system. They will point out the flaws and limitations in the school system and they will provide a perspective that is both valuable and often novel to adults. They often also suggest very reasonable ways to be more valuing and respectful of students' potentially useful ideas.

From the Mouths of Babes

I was asked to lead a discussion of a diverse group of high school students about school improvement. The principal, Bob Dahm (at Belleville Illinois West High School), wisely realized that students' perspectives on his school could be very valuable for him and his teachers to hear. So he assembled a group of students who were representative of the student body (all grades, boys and girls, black and white, jocks and geeks, honor students and failing students, etc.). We were to videotape the conversation to be used to lead small teacher group discussions.

I had not met any of these students before and, since it was a very large school and the students were a cross-section, most did not know each other. As it was my first visit to the school, my first question to them was, "I am new to your school and know very little about it. Can you tell me what it is like? What is its reputation? How would people around here describe it?"

As if they had rehearsed it, they answered almost in unison, "It's a prison!" When I asked why they said that, the answers were "Just look at it. It looks like a prison" (It did. A large multi-story brick block with few windows) and, "If you go outside of the doors during the school day, a group of adults in suits with walkie-talkies will descend on you and drag you back in." (For the uninitiated, those adults are routinely known as High School Assistant Principals.) Then they began to talk about how it is run like a prison. Metal detectors at the entrances. An irrational and overly constrained dress code. How many adults are treated like this at work? And how would we feel if we were?

Educators don't typically realize how wasteful and inefficient it is for them to make all the decisions and solve all the problems in the school. Very frequently, educators who are willing to try empowering students discover that the students (even kindergartners!) have suggestions and solutions that are better than anything the teacher or principal could come up with.

To demonstrate this, I asked the Belleville West high school students, after they justifiably lambasted the overly complex school dress code (which was apparently created and mandated by the School Board), if they could come up with a better one. I was sure they could. Most folks nowadays assume that these kids would want to wear ridiculously, even obscenely, revealing clothing and clothes with antisocial and lewd images on them. Not so. They quickly told me they didn't want to see others' midriffs or thong underwear or girls' tight tube tops. They just wanted a reasonable code. One that was simple and easy to understand and comply with, and one that reflected at least a compromise with what students of their age and at that time would find reasonable attire.

The principal heard this and to his impressive credit (1) anointed this somewhat arbitrary and unorthodox group as his new advisory council and (2) empowered them to create a better dress code. This is exemplary (and sadly rare) school leadership. It shows a respect for students and authentically empowers them. It is the de-prisoning of school.

I have had similar conversations with other focus groups at high schools and middle schools. I even had this conversation once with a group of kindergartners! The best I could get out of them as suggestions for classroom improvement however was "more snacks" and "more recess." But hey, these kids have only been around for five years, and they still showed a reflective desire for having a voice in school improvement, as well as the capacity to make meaningful, albeit egocentric and non-essential, suggestions. And if we want to liberate and nurture student "voice " (which will be addressed more in the next chapter), then we need to start early.

> One of the core functions of schooling in our democratic society is to contribute to the development of the kinds of people needed for our democratic society to survive and thrive. Schools need to foster the acquisition of the knowledge and the development of the skills and dispositions of a responsible, ethical, contributing democratic citizen.

Killing Democracy in Classrooms and Schools

Classroom teachers too need to understand how much they inadvertently oppress their students. Students feel at the mercy of the whims and moods and values and vagaries of their teachers. They know they have no recourse (perhaps other than the relatively toothless "I am going to tell my parents") when teachers act capriciously and unfairly. What are we really teaching students through this hidden curriculum? That they are incompetent? Not to be trusted? That they need adults to control their lives? Is this the kind of student we want to send out to the world as a product of our "education"? I think not.

Now it is important to point out that while teachers in effect may be oppressing students, they are not intentionally doing so. They are decidedly benevolent in their intentions. I don't want to give the impression that I think teachers are intentional despots. Perhaps they are closer to benevolent dictators. And in fact, frequently naïve and self-unaware benevolent dictators. Although, of course, given how many teachers there are in the U.S. alone, there is quite a range of motives and competencies out there. But even if the teacher is caring and benevolent, if he disempowers students, the effect is still the same.

If our society was a dictatorship, even a benevolent dictatorship, then perhaps this would be the perfect educational system to prepare our students for life as adult citizens of such a society. But as we have established earlier, one of the core functions of schooling in our democratic society is to contribute to the development of the kinds of people needed for our democratic society to survive and thrive. Schools need to foster the acquisition of the knowledge and the development of the skills and dispositions of a responsible, ethical, contributing democratic citizen. Schools need to nurture the development of people who understand participation as the bedrock of democracy. People who feel of use and feel competent and want to contribute because they have experienced the value of their contributions. This cannot happen in prison. Schools need to break from the yokes of hierarchical oppression and empower students so they can be the kinds of people we want them to be. The kinds of people we ultimately need them to be.

Hearing Voices: A Pedagogy of Empowerment

Hearing voices has gotten a bad rap. It is usually associated with psycho-pathological delusion, as in "Mrs. Smith, I think we will need to medi-cate your husband because he has been hearing voices." I am not talking about phantom voices, but about unfettering the voices inherent in all of us. Schools need to make space for the authentic voice of its students, indeed for all the members of the school community.

In the preceding chapter, we explored the disempowering nature of too many schools, and even of the entire U.S. educational system from the U.S. Department of Education all the way down to your local classroom. In this chapter, we will introduce an empowering version of schooling, what I call a *pedagogy of empowerment*, and talk about "voice" as the key to unlock that possibility.

Too often noise is confused with nuisance in schools. It is confused with disruption. An impediment to learning. I beg to differ. When I enter a school, I try to sense the pulse, the climate of the school. There are many

> I want to hear the sound of children actively and enthusiastically learning and positively engaging with each other and with the adults in the school.

things I look for. And often I "look" with my ears. I want to hear voices and I want to hear happy, energetic engaged voices. I want to hear the sound of children actively and enthusiastically learning and positively engaging with each other and with the adults in the school. I want to hear and feel positive energy. I don't want to hear...well, nothing. And that is all too often what one hears in a school. Nothing. Certainly in the halls, and frequently in classrooms as students work silently on individual tasks. Of course I am not advocating chaos and cacophony. I understand that there are times and places in the school day where silence is functional and even advantageous. But not most of the time.

The noise level in a school is a metaphor for something deep and fundamental to the human condition. Psychological and philosophical theories discuss the need for a personal sense of meaning, purpose, and a sense of value. Human beings flourish when they feel that they matter; particularly by others who matter to them, but also to everyone. Dan McAdams, a psychologist at Northwestern University, tried to explain the human condition by describing our personalities as a narrative we tell about ourselves. We all have a story of who and what we are (including why we are that way), but it also includes an evaluative theme. Are we good or bad? Are we of value to others and the world in general? Part of a positive self-assessment is feeling that I matter. That includes being "value added"; that is, that I add to the world rather than detract from it. One model of therapy with youth who struggle with drug abuse and/or violence suggests that they need to embrace a philosophy that "I will leave the world a better place than it was when I entered it." In other words, that I will add positive value to the world by virtue of my having spent some time here.

The Destructive Power of Dis-Empowerment

Victor Frankl, in the remarkable chronicle of his journey to survive Nazi concentration camps (and his ensuing theory of psychotherapy and personality), argued that "man's search for meaning" (the title of his book) is a fundamental aspect of the human experience. At the heart of his ability to survive when he had no freedom was his search for something important he still could control. In his case, it was his attitude. I know of more than one high school teacher who used Frankl's notion and discovery to help their high school students learn to control their attitudes, yet another connection between prisons and schools as we established in the preceding chapter.

This notion of self-control has been found to be a remarkably potent factor in the human experience in many areas of psychology. In the field of health psychology, it has been found not only to be linked to positive mental health, but also to physical wellness and healing (for example, in recuperation from surgery or a heart attack). The sense of a lack of control has been called "learned helplessness" by Martin Seligman and linked to depression. Philosophers often call this sense of having no control over one's life an existential crisis. Having a sense of control over one's life and its context is part of being human and contributes heavily to mental and physical well-being, to human flourishing. Interestingly, Seligman's journey has moved from his focus on depression and learned helplessness due to a lack of control to the study of optimism and, the title of his new book, *Flourishing*, in what he calls the field of "positive psychology."

So what does this have to do with voice and empowerment? One important way to have control and feel that one has control is to have influence. I don't mean the kind of influence that major societal and global power brokers do. I simply mean that I know that I have the potential of influencing what happens to and around me. And one way of knowing that is by seeing how my voice is welcome, invited, respected, heard, and considered seriously. When I know that my teachers or fellow students (or my parents or older siblings, etc.), want to know my opinion and that they will seriously listen to it, then I know there is a possibility that my voice may influence what happens. So I feel valued. My voice matters.

Doing It Right

As we saw in the last chapter, schools are often more likely to stifle voices than to liberate them, and more likely to dis-empower than to empower. One of the videos I use in teacher professional development is a real-life capture of a kindergarten teacher managing a conflict between two five-year-old boys. It comes from the Child Development Project of the Developmental Studies Center and is called "two boys and one chair." The teacher, Linda Rayford, encounters Peter and Ray (pseudonyms) who decide they both want to sit in the same chair, in an activity where each child is supposed to choose a chair and decorate the paper plate that has been put in front of each chair. Most teachers would simply engineer a solution to this momentary disruption of classroom order, but Rayford knows that problems are opportunities in disguise and sees the chance to use developmental discipline to promote Peter and Ray's character development. She notes and names the problem and then asks them to "work it out" and walks away.

When she revisits and finds that they have been unable to resolve the problem, she becomes Socrates and engages in discussion with them to help them solve it. She continually resists solving it herself. Here alone she is giving them control and making space for their voices. But the matter of voice doesn't stop there in this case. While she is talking with them, another boy at their table, Mike, chimes in and says, "I know a solution. You share." He is suggesting that they share the plate and collaborate on decorating it, rather than, as instructed and as the task is defined, each have their own plate.

It is not the suggested solution on which I want to focus here. Rather it is what Rayford did. Most teachers would never have given these two five-year-old boys the freedom (and control) to solve this problem. But even those who would have done so would likely not have been very accepting of Mike's uninvited interjection. How often have you uttered the following reprimands: "Mind your own business," "Don't you have your own work to do?" I think in the case of Peter and Ray, most teachers would have seen Mike's interjection as a complication of the problem and would redirect Mike with something like, "Don't you have your own plate to decorate?" But not Linda Rayford, for she understands the value of voice and autonomy and she supported Mike's suggestion, which in fact became the operative solution to the problem and worked very nicely.

Edward Deci and Richard Ryan's self-determination theory promotes what they call autonomy-supportive classrooms; that is, classrooms that are structured to honor student voice. Their extensive research over decades demonstrates the powerful influence of supporting student autonomy on both classroom climate and many positive student outcomes, including character development and academic achievement.

Making space for student voice is central to many character education programs that have been shown to have significant positive influences on student development and learning: Child Development Project (now called Caring School Community), Open Circle, Responsive Classroom, Just Community Schools. These well-crafted and effective programs institutionalize student voice through class meetings, morning meetings, community meetings, and in many other ways.

But it is not just through formal programs that this can happen. About a year ago, I was visiting one of my favorite elementary schools, Mark Twain Elementary in Brentwood, Missouri. I was taking a visitor on a tour of this

National School of Character and we were hosted by the principal, Karen Smith, one of the best elementary school principals I have known. She is also one of the most empowering educators and seems to naturally value others' voices. One of their initiatives is "families." Families are vertical groupings of students (two kindergartners, two first graders, two second graders, etc.) with an adult. In this school, ALL adults participate: all teachers, but also the principal, her secretary, the cook, etc. Everyone matters at Mark Twain. One of the ways that Mark Twain makes kids matter is to give them meaningful responsibilities. On family day, the fourth graders are charged with fetching their kindergarten family members and bringing them to the meetings. The fifth-graders actually lead the family character lessons.

This last responsibility was new last year and so it had only happened for a few months when I was visiting. So we went up to Jonathon Lee's fifth grade classroom to ask the kids about how it was going. When Karen asked, we received some charming answers. "It is really hard. You can't get kindergartners to do what you tell them!" "We went on a field trip and one of the kindergartners fell asleep in my lap and I didn't know what to do!" It was at that point that the devil got the better of me (as he often does when I visit schools and classrooms). So I said to the students: "Guys, it sounds like you have learned a lot about being a teacher over the last three months. But you have also watched Mr. Lee teaching you for three months. I bet you have some good advice for him on how he can do an even better job of teaching you." (It is important to note that I knew Jonathon Lee and was fairly confident that he would be open to this discussion.)

They took my question/invitation quite seriously and the ensuing discussion was brilliant. First they pointed out what Jonathon does that is effective. They told him what he does that helps them understand, that makes them enjoy learning, that helps them perform well on tests, pay attention, and so on. And then they pointed out some things he does that make it harder to remember or learn or test well.

Frankly, I think every teacher should have this mid-year discussion with his or her students. Students have a unique and powerful window on what is working and what is not. Why would any teacher not want to know how to teach his or her students more effectively? I firmly believe that if this specific form of making a place for student voice happened in every classroom, then American education would leap ahead in terms of effectiveness.

This is but one example of voice for one set of stakeholders. Teachers need voice as well. Far too many administrators waste (ignore, stifle, discount) the voices of the adults in the building. Just look at the typical faculty meeting in a school. It looks like 19th century education! Principal in front of the room reading a list of announcements. But I will return to this later.

So think about the deep and fundamental role of voice in the human experience (oh, and yeah, students are humans, too, by the way). Think of how empowerment and autonomy promote positive development of character and learning. And how schools are so like prisons in thwarting autonomy, in stifling voices, and in disempowering all. And they don't have to be and shouldn't be. Do you want to be prison guard? Or can you be the liberator of student voice and the uplifter of the fundamental human spirit of students? The choice is yours. Really.

Being Your Own Best Teacher

Education is pervasively misaligned. By that I mean that there is a lack of fit between what teachers know and typically value and what teachers do. They fail to align their practices with their educational philosophies. I have met teachers who eloquently advocate for and explain the virtues of constructivist education, student empowerment, discovery learning, child-centered education, differentiated instruction, developmental discipline, and other enlightened pedagogies, and then observed them relying on exactly the opposite approach to teaching their students and managing their classrooms.

I once observed a teacher who taught her peers how to lead democratic class meetings and then led such meetings in her own classroom with a didactic, authoritarian style that disempowered her students. I suspected that I had been had by a stellar con-artist. But I realized that was not the case. In fact, she *thought* she was empowering students, being democratic, and following the best principles of class meeting management. She just did not realize the lack of correspondence between her beliefs and assumptions and her practices. Now you might think that she represented an aberration. You may assume that she is a rare case to be studied for its uniqueness. Far from it. In fact she is typical, and not just among educators. Humans tend not to be adequately introspective, and when they are, they are rarely objective in their self-analyses and observations.

In other words, we don't know ourselves as well as we think we do, and that can lead to substantial self-distortions and misconceptions. Many of you are at least loosely familiar with Howard Gardner's notion of *multiple intelligences*. One of the nine intelligences we have is called *intrapersonal intelligence* and it refers to our ability to be self-reflective and generate a deep and accurate understanding of ourselves. Some of us are good at this and others are not. As teachers, if we are not high in intrapersonal intelligence, then we can misunderstand what kind of teacher we are and what our capabilities are. But all of us can at times think we are one kind of teacher and be quite another kind, without realizing it at all. I find this to be a very common problem among teachers in regard to their sense of themselves as educators. So each of us may be off target in judging how and how well we function as an educator (teacher, administrator, etc.) or, for that matter, as a parent or neighbor, etc.

Another team of psychologists, Christopher Argyris and Donald Schoen, introduced the distinction between *espoused theory* and *theory in action*. What this represents in the difference between what you claim to be your theory or philosophy (espoused theory) and what seems to be behind the actual choices you make and behaviors you engage in (theory in action). The point is that we may, even very convincingly and eloquently, say that we think children flourish and learn best when loved and supported (our espoused theory) but then frequently resort to humiliation and punishment when things are not going as we hoped (theory in action).

One framework for this problem is to think in term of "mental models." A mental model is a theory you have about the world. It may be explicit; that is, you may have thought about it and even described it. Or it may be implicit; that is, it may clearly describe how you operate, but you have never reflected on it and may not even be aware of it. An analogy is how we learn and use grammar. For our primary and first language, we learn grammar at an age and developmental level when we really could not understand or explain it. We continue to apply grammar in a complex and accurate way, but if asked how we make such choices, probably do not know and could not explain it. One question I like to ask teachers is, "What is your mental model of what changes a person's character?" Because most teachers have not thought about this. Often the methods they most readily employ (rewards, public affirmations, exhortations like posters and quotations) are far from what they theoretically would postulate as significant forces in character formation, as was discussed in Chapter 5.

What Educators Say They Should Do and Actually Do

A few years ago, the national organization for character education in the U.S., the Character Education Partnership (www.character.org), did a national survey of educators who were connected to the field of character education. One of the things they asked them was "what do you think influences character development in students?" The three strongest influences named in this survey were:

> We seem to know (espoused theory) what truly works, but are not likely to implement those things in our schools (theory in action).

- Opportunities to develop caring, positive relationships with peers and school staff (chosen by 74% as one of their top three)

- Opportunities to be of service to others in school and community (60%)

- Opportunities to discuss ethical issues embedded in academic schoolwork (42%).

The lowest two (of nine strategies) were:

- Awards programs that publicly recognize students who manifest good character (only 17% put that in their top three)

- Posters, announcements, and motivational speakers that publicize good character (9%).

Yet when these same educators were asked "which of the following statements best characterize(s) your school's/district's current predominant efforts to promote character development?" the answers were very different:

- Two-thirds of the educators identified "publicizing virtues and values in the school (assemblies, announcements, wall postings)"

- Over half identified "visible recognition and reward programs"

- But less than half identified service learning (40%) or "comprehensive range of activities (CE in academic activities and governance" (43%).

In other words, we seem to know (espoused theory) what truly works, but are not likely to implement those things in our schools (theory in action).

> **What Educators Say They Should Do and What They Say They Actually Do to Influence Character** (From the Character Education Partnership)
>
> - **What Educators Say they Should Do (Top Three)**
>   - Create opportunities to develop caring, positive relationships with peers and school staff
>   - Create opportunities to be of service to others
>   - Create opportunities to discuss ethical issues in schoolwork
>
> - **What Educators Say They Should Do (Bottom Two)**
>   - Awards programs for public recognition of student character
>   - Posters, announcements and motivational speakers
>
> - **What Educators Say They Actually Do Most Frequently**
>   - Publicizing virtues and values through assemblies, announcements and wall postings
>   - Visible recognition and reward programs

Learning from Our Best and Worst Teachers

So what can we do to rectify this problem of alignment, to make mental models more explicit and to check on whether they are justifiable and whether our practices align with them? There are two parts to the solution to the problem of alignment. The first is to better articulate the kind of teacher you want to be. Surely, we do some of this in our teacher education programs at our schools and colleges of education. But (1) you are a real novice at that point and are in little position to conceptualize and articulate your sense of an ideal teacher and (2), as we have argued already, it is not done that well anyhow (don't get me started on how poorly we prepare teachers in the USA; that is the subject for another book). This articulation needs to be done incrementally throughout one's career, being adapted, amended and readjusted as one has more experience, matures as a person, and can better understand the profession of education. So on-the-job training (in-service professional education) becomes important in order to effectively tackle this educational trap.

One of my favorite in-service exercises is "Best Teacher/Worst Teacher." It goes like this: (1) Get a group of educators together (often the staff of a single school). (2) Create two equal circles; an inner circle and an outer circle, with the inner facing outward and the outer facing inward so the two circles form a set of pairs facing each other. (3) Have the pairs greet each other and then have each member of the pair share a description of his or her favorite teacher from when he or she was a student. Be sure to have them state the teacher's name as a form of tribute. Each member of the pair gets a chance to share. (4) Have them thank and say goodbye to their partners and then ask one of the circles to rotate (e.g., inner circle moves three people to the left or outer circle moves two people to the right, etc.). (5) Have them greet their new partners and then have each partner share the worst teacher he or she has ever had (while still a student), or the worst memory of how a teacher treated him or her in a particular instance. This time be sure that they keep the teacher anonymous. (6) Then have them thank their partners and all return to their seats.

The most important part of this exercise is what follows: group reflection. Start with the "Best Teacher." Ask the group to share some of the stories of the best teachers (on a volunteer basis). Ask individuals to share their own stories or the stories they heard from their partners (with the permission of their partners, of course). When a story is told, ask the person to say the name of the teacher and what grade and/or subject he or she taught. Point out that this is a testimony to that excellent teacher. While this is happening, keep a running written list (on a chalkboard, flip chart, overhead, etc.) of the central characteristics that made each teacher so precious and memorable; for example, "she saw potential in me."

Next turn the reflection portion to the "Worst Teacher." The only difference is to ask the educators not to use names or identifying information, as they are giving negative information about others. Keep a new list of what the "worst teachers" did that led to their being so memorable.

The last step is to help them process what can be learned from these stories and reflections. First, I go over each list separately building a cumulative picture of the best and worst teacher (more on this below). Then, I ask them if they have ever told their best teacher how they value him or her. I point out what a tribute it is to them and they should know it. I also make the point that they have just cumulatively defined the ideal teacher from their

The Best Teacher/Worst Teacher Exercise

Step 1. Assemble the staff (or some other group of at least 20 educators).

Step 2. Ask them to form a circle and count off by twos.

Step 3. Ask the "2"s to take a step forward, turn around and form an inner circle.

Step 4. Ask each person to find a partner across from them. (If there is an odd number, then either "yoke" two members or have the facilitator join in.)

Step 5. Ask them to greet their partner, and if they don't already know each other, to meet their partner.

Step 6. Ask each person to identify and describe the best teacher that he or she had as a student; and to explain why that teacher was their favorite. (Ask them to share the name and job of the identified teacher.)

Step 7. When all have shared (it usually takes only a couple of minutes), get their attention and tell them to (a) thank their partners and (b) say goodbye to their partners.

Step 8. Ask one of the circles to rotate three or four people to the left.

Step 9. Instruct each person to meet and greet their new partner.

Step 10. Instruct each person to share the story of the worst teacher he or she had as a student. (Be sure to tell them to be anonymous—no indentifying information.)

Step 11. Ask them to thank and say goodbye to their partners and return to their seats.

Step 12. Ask for voluntary sharing of best teacher stories; record the key characteristics of those teachers on a flip chart. (Ask them to say the names of those teachers to honor them.)

Step 13. Ask for voluntary sharing of worst teacher stories; record the key characteristics of those teachers on a separate sheet of flip chart paper. (Remind them not to give any identifying information.)

Process the two lists:

a. Ask them if they have ever told their best teacher.

b. Point out that they have cumulatively defined great teaching and terrible teaching.

c. Note that nearly none of the characteristics are about content knowledge.

d. Ask administrators what they do to move all of their teachers further from the worst list and closer to the best list.

e. Ask them if they would want someone to nominate them for the best teacher activity and what they are doing to make it happen.

own experiences as students. They have, as a group, identified the best and worst characteristics and practices of teachers. This in fact is a recipe for success (or failure).

When working with administrators, which I often do, I also then ask a rather daunting question, "If this is what you want every one of your teachers to be, what are you doing every day to make that happen?" I tell them that they need to be strategically and intentionally doing whatever is necessary to help every teacher in their schools to move closer to the ideal and away from the worst teacher model. Finally, I return to the best teacher concept and the idea of saying their names as testimonials or tributes. And I ask one last daunting question, "I did not create this exercise nor am I the only one who does it in workshops. Some of you may have in fact done a version of this before. And others may be doing this same exercise right now somewhere else. Perhaps even in this town. Wouldn't you like it if someone were saying your name right now when identifying his or her favorite teacher? What are you doing to make that happen?"

What is most revealing to me about this exercise is that (1) it generates nearly the same characteristics each time, (2) it seems a revelation to educators, and (3) there is very little, if anything, in either list about a teacher's knowledge of academic content or her pedagogical training or prowess. Instead it tends to be almost exclusively about how those teachers treat people, what kinds of people they are, and generally about their character. So let's take a look at what teachers generate when reflecting on their best and worst teachers.

Characteristics of Our Best Teachers

Favorite teachers are singled out time and time again for the following characteristics (and I have done this exercise many times): Favorite teachers are teachers who:

- **Build personal relationships with students.** Teachers often describe a former teacher who took an interest in him or her on a more personal level. Sometimes it is because of a common interest (e.g., chess, stamp collecting, or sports statistics). Sometimes it is simply social chemistry; the teacher seemed to like the student and reached out (often because the teacher sensed the student needed emotional support). Often a catalyst for this is the teacher's self-disclosure (telling the student about herself and her life). Simply getting to know each other is a step in this direction. Charlie Abourjilie, author of *Developing Character for Classroom Success*, is a high school/middle school teacher and he would create an autobiographical niche in his room so students could learn more about him. Teacher Kim McConnell, from Walt Disney Elementary in California, begins the year by letting students interview her about her life and interests and background. What is especially intriguing about this is that it also fits the Pedagogy of Empowerment, because rather than simply telling the students what she wants them to know, she allows them to control the puppet strings for a moment and decide what they want to know (of course she reserves the right not to answer any question she chooses not to answer, but that almost is never necessary).

- **Make learning (and classrooms) fun.** My favorite teacher was Mr. Sloan, my sixth-grade (elementary school) teacher. Mr. Sloan was a WWII combat veteran, and a big burly man (at least from the perspective of my sixth-grade eyes). Because of space constraints, my sixth grade class was housed in the junior high school (which normally only housed seventh and eighth graders), so we were a bit overwhelmed by our location, social context etc. But Mr. Sloan was our rock. We felt safe with him. That, however, is not the only reason I remember him so fondly. It was because he not only expected us to learn and perform at high levels (see the next characteristic), but he made our potentially daunting year in the junior high school fun. For instance, he taught us to march military style (including turning corners sharply) whenever we moved through the halls as a class. He would toss the eraser at us (gently) if he thought were weren't paying attention, but we knew we were allowed to throw it back at him (also gently) if we thought he was day-dreaming. He joked with us constantly, but all in the context of learning. I still remember moments of hysterics in that class as we were allowed to be really silly while doing class presentations around curricular material; e.g., we totally wrapped one of our fellow students in toilet paper to create a "mummy" for our reenactment of Egyptian history that we were studying. The entire class was hysterical when we carried this good sport into the room for our little drama. I also recall

Mr. Sloan astounding us with the fact that he and his fellow soldiers were not allowed to drink from the public wells in Italian towns because they would get sick, but the Italian children could drink the same water and be unaffected. We thought it amazing that U.S. soldiers in general and our rock of a combat veteran teacher were "weaker" than the local children. Hal Urban reports in his book *Lessons from the Classroom* that he institutionalized humor in his high school classrooms, both by collecting and sharing funny stories and by asking students to do likewise.

> Too often people think that students prefer the easy teacher, but I have found that people remember and revere the teacher who benevolently held them to a higher standard.

- **Set high standards (expect high performance).** Students typically value teachers who push them to perform in ways they didn't think they could previously. Teachers remember the teacher that showed them how well they could do in school by expecting more and not settling for less. Such teachers' stories are so compelling that Hollywood has repeatedly chosen them as the basis for major motion pictures: Jaime Escalante in *Stand and Deliver* or Erin Gruell in *Freedom Writers*. Oftentimes the stories educators tell are about the teacher who motivated them ultimately to become a teacher. Too often people think that students prefer the easy teacher, but I have found that people remember and revere the teacher who benevolently held them to a higher standard. In fact, I went into developmental psychology and became a professor because my undergraduate developmental psychology professor, Willis Overton, taught such a high level class and included us in the development of a highly complex and ultimately influential theory he was working on. He had us grappling with high level concepts and reading source level material. And that really turned me on to the richness of developmental psychology.

- **Model a passion for learning and knowledge.** Following this notion of teachers inspiring students to become teachers, are tales of teachers who built a passion for learning in students. One middle school math teacher voraciously reads books written for middle school students and then tells her math students about them, because she had a teacher who loved reading, shared that with students, and inspired them to love reading as well. Many schools require or allow teachers to run clubs about topics of particular interest to them (e.g., chess, computer programming). One National School of Character, St. Genevieve High School in Panorama California, ends every day with every student taking physical education. But in this case, each teacher is required to lead a physical education class in an area of physical exercise that is personally important to them (e.g., jogging, aerobics, speed walking, rope jumping, martial arts, and yoga). They expect all students to be fit and are willing to go beyond the norm to create the scaffolding to make this more likely.

- **See potential in students that others don't see.** Despite the title of "No Child Left Behind," far too many students fall through the cracks of our schools. I am not just referring to the markedly failing students or the Tarnished Kids introduced in Chapter 3, rather I mean any student who is performing at a level significantly below their potential. Schools often don't recognize what students are capable of. As we argued earlier they don't see the possibilities in each child. Sometimes teachers just don't care about a particular student or group of students (or in some cases, sadly, any students). Sometimes students get mislabeled, or get a reputation for the wrong reasons or for reasons that are simply inaccurate. I recall hearing a lecture by a National Teacher of the Year who described himself as on a track for failure and dropout. He came from a family besieged by alcoholism and obesity. He was obese himself and did not care about learning and did not believe he could succeed academically. One teacher, however, saw potential in him, reached out to him, and invited him to join the student newspaper staff. This turned his life around and led

> Part of Edward Deci and Richard Ryan's *self-determination theory* is the argument that a sense of competence is a fundamental human need that schools need to serve.

> **Commonly Reported Characteristics of Best Teachers**
> - They build personal relationships with students.
> - They make classrooms and learning fun.
> - They set high standards and expect high performance.
> - The model a passion for learning and knowledge.
> - They see potential in students that others don't see.
> - They go above and beyond the standard boundaries of the normal school day.

him to become not only a teacher, but a remarkable teacher recognized for excellence on a national level. Every student (indeed every one of us) needs to feel competent. Part of Edward Deci and Richard Ryan's self-determination theory is the argument that a sense of competence is a fundamental human need that schools need to serve. Schools need to strategically find a place for each student to be competent and to feel competent. For most it is some area of academics. For many it is athletics or the arts or music. But for some, the talents are hidden or non-traditional. And the best educators find them and honor them and nurture them. They make space in the life of the school for them. B.R. Rhoads, an exemplary elementary school principal tells the story of a very troubled fifth-grade boy who he was failing to reach. Part of his ultimate success was first getting to know the boy better (building relationships) and then discovering and nurturing two of his talents: computers and yo-yos. This not only served his need for competency, but it also helped build positive relationships with other students once they saw his talents.

- **Go above and beyond the standard constraints of the school day for students.** I have had the good fortune of working with three former middle school principals (Beverly Nance, Kristen Pelster, and Tim Crutchley) who would routinely go to the homes of chronically tardy or absent students to wake them and get them out of bed and to school on time. Pelster also periodically does the laundry of poor families at her school. And they are just some of the thousands of educators who do those and similar services for their students and the families of their students every day. Other teachers have described fellow teachers who invited students to their homes. Loraine Monroe, a highly regarded master educator from Harlem in New York City, described an after school girls' social she hosted in her apartment, where inner city minority teens would learn manners, how to dress properly for social circumstances, how to have sophisticated civil conversations about current events, etc. She did this to give them a greater chance at success in life.

Characteristics of Our Worst Teachers

So now that we have seen some of the key ingredients of the "best teachers," let's take a closer look at the "worst teachers" who are less complex to describe:

- **They are mean to students, often for categorical reasons** (e.g., race, ethnicity, gender, religion, and appearance). Teachers often relate a single moment in their careers as students when a teacher minimized them because of their appearance, socio-economic status, race, religion, etc. Such teachers tell students that they will not succeed in school and/or life because of gender or race, etc. Often they will scoff at a student's aspirations.

> I often tell educators that if there is one thing they learn from me, it is to never again publicly humiliate a child (or anyone else for that matter).

- **They humiliate students publicly.** Teachers often relate memories of moments in the classroom when a teacher made fun of them in front of the class for saying something wrong, speaking incorrectly, etc. This may in fact be the single most powerfully negative thing that a teacher can do to a student. I often tell educators that if there is one thing they learn from me, it is to never again publicly humiliate a child (or anyone else for that matter). These are the stories that are most likely to reduce a teacher to tears when telling about his "worst teacher" moment, even when that moment occurred 40 or 50 years ago! It is fine to reprimand a student when it is earned, and even to show strong emotions while doing so. But one never needs an audience to reprimand a child. Never.

- **They are insensitive to student pain, crisis, etc.** I have heard countless tales of teachers disregarding a student's emotional state, personal life crisis, etc. Teachers tell of their teachers refusing to make allowances on a test or assignment despite a painful loss of a loved one, for example. As noted in Chapter 2, students cannot shed their lives when they come to school and often those lives are so overpowering that students cannot be reasonably expected to function effectively in school. Teachers need to understand and make accommodations for that harsh reality. And as surrogate parents, students need teachers who care about and for them. Not just as part of a group or class, but as unique individuals.

- **They are rigid, inflexible, and unfair.** Many tales of least favorite teachers are about patterns of favoritism and bias on the one hand and rigidity and inflexibility on the other hand. Teachers are described as having class pets. (I even worked with a professor who routinely had a teacher's pet and a class scapegoat at the graduate seminar level! It was incredibly destructive of student morale and effective teaching.) Teachers are described who refuse to bend rules even when circumstances clearly call for adaptability. The sense of injustice is palpable when teachers report on a worst teacher who refused to accommodate the unique characteristics of their plight.

- **They simply don't seem to care about students and/or teaching.** I have heard many stories of teachers who seemed bored with teaching or even voiced jaundiced treatises on the pointlessness of teaching. And I have heard many other stories of teachers who made it painfully clear that they disdained most or all students.

Commonly Reported Characteristics of Worst Teachers
- They are mean to students.
- They publicly humiliate students.
- They are blind or insensitive to student pain and crisis.
- They are rigid, inflexible, and unfair.
- They don't seem to care about students and/or teaching.

What is most remarkable to me about the "Worst Teacher" stories is how salient and painful they remain, often after many decades, even half a century. As noted in Chapter 7 on Jedi Teaching, I have seen teachers cry as they describe a single incident that occurred in a classroom 20, 30, 40, or even more years in the past. The pain seems not to diminish over the years. These are often the same teachers who feel impotent and disregarded by students, who wonder if they make a difference. This exercise is a powerful way to bring home the power that every teacher has, as we have already discussed.

The Power of Reflection and Feedback

Reflection is the first missing ingredient in increasing the alignment of teacher values and philosophy with their actual practice. Teachers need to develop a clearer picture of the kind of teacher they want to be (and the kind they do not want to be). But there is a second ingredient. It is feedback. Teachers need a mirror in which they can see what they are really like as educators. Remember that problem of alignment? It was built in large part because of how little accurate knowledge we have about the kinds of teachers we are.

There are numerous ways of gaining this knowledge. Every teacher should be observed by a supervisor (principal, department head, etc.) and given performance feedback. Certainly we can also now rely on technology and can videotape teachers so they can see themselves in action (boy do I hate that one, but it is like taking one's medicine...it may taste nasty, but it works). For many, however, this is not materially feasible or too emotionally threatening.

Another way to gain insight into one's own practices is to build in peer feedback. When Cynthia Whitaker was principal at Lexington Elementary in the St. Louis Public Schools, she created an expectation that every teacher would spend at least a minute or two (and ideally longer) in another teacher's classroom every school day. Procedurally it was simple to enact as teachers could drop in on each others' classrooms when going to or from lunch, after dropping off their students in art or music, etc. In this way, each teacher cumulatively sampled much of their peers' normal practice over the course of a school year. All those few seemingly trivial minutes of peer observation each day ultimately added up to hours of peer observation over the course of a school year. What needs to be added, however, is a formal mechanism for discussing what they observed.

More formally, mentor teachers serve this purpose, as can middle school academic team peers, or high school academic department members. Clearly when team teaching occurs such as in cross-age buddying programs, there is ample opportunity for peer feedback. The real challenge is creating a staff culture where such feedback is expected, safe, productive, and eventually welcomed for professional growth. The school (and/or district) leadership is critical to creating such a professional learning community culture. In some schools, this is informal but in others it is done formally (as in schools adopting Rick Dufour's *Professional Learning Community* model, or following the suggestions in Chapter 4 of Lickona and Davidson's *Smart and Good High Schools*). We will return to the issue of the adult culture of the school in Chapter 17.

Another powerful and helpful source of feedback that is almost always overlooked is students. At the university level we routinely ask students to rate professors' teaching effectiveness. In fact, now there are websites that, like other consumer reports, provide such evaluations. (This is admittedly fraught with perils, but the general idea of gathering student evaluations is a good one.) In a sense students are consumers, disempowered consumers. This is more apparent at the private school or post-secondary level where one directly pays for one's education. But we all pay for public education, so it is true there as well.

Ways to Get Feedback on One's Teaching

- Have a supervisor observe you and provide feedback.
- Ask a peer to observe you and provide feedback.
- Ask your mentor to observe you and provide feedback.
- Ask your students for advice on what to continue, change and stop.

Students can help immensely by providing feedback on what they feel helps them learn and helps them want to learn, and what does not. Sadly, those voices are rarely heard by teachers. I always asked my undergraduate students to fill out an anonymous evaluation as a supplement to the required university evaluation to let me know what they think I should stop doing, keep doing, and change doing. It has been immensely helpful to me over the years and I frequently altered my practices when I believed the student input was valid and productive, which it frequently is.

> All of our schools would be better places if we could get all teachers to reflect on the kind of teacher they want to be, get an accurate picture of the kind of teacher they currently are, and move to bridge the gap between the two.

Clearly the last ingredient in solving the alignment problem is to motivate teachers to reflect on the gap between their goals and values and their actual practice. This must be part of school culture. The school leader is critical to making this happen. She needs to expect it and to model it herself, and to create the context, opportunity, and even possibility of it happening. One principal reported that he has all teachers keep a guided structured journal and he read and responded to each entry in each journal.

One new teacher was lamenting to me recently that she was frightened and didn't know how to structure her class. Part of my advice was to become the teacher she would want to have. A seasoned kindergarten teacher once told me that she likes to stop at some point each afternoon and ask herself how she could have done the day better. I think that is an example of simple brilliance and clearly is personally institutionalizing professional reflection. All of our schools would be better places if we could get all teachers to reflect on the kind of teacher they want to be, get an accurate picture of the kind of teacher they currently are, and move to bridge the gap between the two.

The Brain Drain

We are a very wasteful society. I try to do my best by recycling at home and wherever such a system is available. I know it is only a drop in the proverbial bucket, but at least I feel that I am doing something to avoid waste. I actually feel good each week when I wheel out the recycling cart to the curb and feel how heavy it is with all the paper and bottles and cans that I am sending to be reused in some cosmic cycle rather than simply sending it off to a garbage dump.

I am aware how wasteful we are as a society. However, I do have my limits. I was not willing to go so far as to use cloth diapers when my son was a baby. I felt guilty about adding to the vast piles of waste across the land, but couldn't muster the fortitude to deal with more literal buckets of soiled diapers for years. And I realize that I was simply adding to the waste and pollution of our world. I know somewhere there is a small mountain of my garbage, my son's diapers, my many discarded computers and other electrical appliances, my old car tires, etc. It probably has a plaque with my name on it: Mt. Marvin.

But what I really want to talk about here is a different sort of waste. Waste that happens in schools. Not the sort you think, either. Certainly there is plenty of material waste in our schools. In fact, one caring and resourceful student in Florida managed to get a law passed allowing Florida schools to send left over lunch food to homeless shelters. The law had apparently prohibited that (assumedly for health reasons) and this student saw the illogic in people going hungry while schools were discarding perfectly good food. Problems like that are plentiful (and kids like him are unfortunately in less abundance; however, to see more stories of people who stick their necks out to serve others' needs like this Florida student, check out the Giraffe Heroes Project at www.giraffe.org).

But the waste I am talking about in schools is the waste of brainpower. Call it Brain Drain. It is as if there is a big drain in the center of every school and great ideas and brain power are continually flowing across the floors of our schools and down the drains, rather than being used and applied and harvested.

Wasting Teacher's Best Practices...and Brains

I will share two glaring examples of this chronic brain drain. The first example is the waste of teachers' best practices. It is my opinion that all teachers, even the few really lousy teachers who I would prefer would leave the teaching profession, do something clever. Something creative and effective. Something brilliant. All teachers figure out ways of delivering lessons, evaluating students, managing behavior, decorating and arranging the classroom, having fun, getting to know students, involving parents, etc. And some of those are poor, some are mediocre, and some are great.

> When teachers construe good pedagogy as proprietary, then students lose and education is impoverished.

But only a very few of those ideas and methods are actually shared with their colleagues at all. And if they are shared, it is likely to be informally and on a very limited basis, rather than strategically, effectively, and systematically shared with all who could benefit and in ways that they could optimally benefit. Teachers simply don't share best practices on a routine basis. It is as if a teacher surreptitiously slinks into her classroom and secretly executes her teaching plan, sometimes brilliantly, with no one else knowing what she does.

In *Change Leadership*, Tony Wagner, Bob Kegan, and their colleagues conclude that schools have evolved to be a culture of silos, where teachers expect to (and are expected to) rule over their individual fiefdoms (classrooms) in isolation from one another and from their supervisors. Of course teachers talk to each other informally and formally about teaching. There are department meetings, staff meetings, team meetings, etc. And of course, administrators observe and evaluate teaching. And sometimes they even do those evaluations well and provide meaningful feedback...to the individual teacher. No one else is privy to the observation and the feedback in the vast majority of cases.

But I am talking about a much more intentional and systematic form of sharing best practices. Some folks, like my colleague Tom Lickona, make it a deliberate practice to collect and disseminate best practices. Tom originally wanted to be a sports reporter and did so for a while, so his orientation to education is to find, collect, and report on the good work that others do, and he does it eloquently and effectively (see particularly his books: *Educating for Character*, *Character Matters*, and *Smart and Good High Schools*).

Others, such as Hal Urban, author of *Lessons from the Classroom*, intentionally disseminate the best practices they developed in their years in their own classroom silos. Hal taught for 35 years in two Bay Area high schools, but never had administrative support for the brilliant practices he was creating in implementing in his classrooms; nor did he experience interest and support from his fellow teachers. Hal reports that a fellow teacher was approached by a student who innocently and sincerely suggested he adopt a particularly popular and effective practice that Hal had created and implemented in his classrooms. She asked the teacher, "How come you don't greet us at the door like Mr. Urban does?" He put her down for suggesting it and put Hal down for his practice. In fact this teacher made a point to tell Hal later that Hal tried too hard to be popular with the kids. As Hal notes, that teacher "was unpopular with the students but cocky and thought he had all the answers." Brain drain, indeed.

> Education should be a communal effort to serve all children, not a competition to see which teacher can be better than her peers.

Why are teachers so unlikely to allow their great innovations to venture out into the light of day? There are many reasons, including the overly packed schedule leaving no time for teacher sharing. But a few others are more disheartening. One common refrain I hear from teachers is that teachers hesitate to describe an innovation that is working well because "others will think I am bragging." That is very sad. It is almost an epitaph for the adult culture in those schools (see Chapter 17), and in a related way, a condemnation of leadership in those schools (see Chapter 16).

But it gets worse. The other common explanation I hear is that "others might steal my ideas." When teachers construe good pedagogy as proprietary, then students lose and education is impoverished. And when teachers see their colleagues as thieves and threats, then the entire adult culture of the school and consequently the whole school culture is impaired. Education should be a communal effort to serve all children, not a competition to see which teacher can be better than her peers. Sadly, the entire federal effort to improve U.S. education, most notably the core accountability strategies of the No Child Left Behind legislation from the Bush administration and the Obama administration's Race to the Top and focus on merit pay, only serve to promote such a "silo-ed" and competitive orientation to education.

The last cause of this non-sharing brain drain propensity in schools is that school leaders seem not to recognize that it is part of their job description to intentionally and strategically create the context and motivation for educators to routinely share best practices. Earlier I described how elementary school principal Cynthia Whitaker institutionalized daily staff peer observations. Another elementary school principal, Renee Goodman, turned her staff meetings into class meetings where open sharing routinely could occur, rather than the absurd didactic meetings where most principals read a bunch of announcements to their staff, thereby both wasting staff community time and modeling horrendous pedagogy as the instructional leaders of their staff.

So what I urge schools to do is to institutionalize the sharing of best practices. Some principals have now added a sharing of best practices to every faculty meeting agenda. Some do a periodic "show and tell" where teachers describe and even demonstrate a favored practice. Many schools are creating formal (e.g., Professional Learning Communities) or informal (e.g., friendship circles or book groups) teacher groups to talk about teaching. As Gus Jacobs of the Kansas City Basic School Network says "when teachers talk to teachers about teaching, good things happen for children."

When I was a member of the psychology department at Marquette University, we each were assigned about 20–30 undergraduate psychology majors to advise. We were expected to meet with each one individually at least twice a year to plan courses for the upcoming semester (and beyond), check on progress, and offer career and/or graduate school advice. At one point we realized that there was no guidance, training, regulation, or evaluation of advising. We were each winging it and, given informal and unsolicited feedback from students, some were doing much better at advising than were others.

So I suggested we have a faculty meeting at which everyone would share one advising practice they used that they thought was particularly helpful. It might entail a system for making appointments, or a form of record keeping, or a set of questions used during advising, etc. In fact, this session, which was unprecedented for this group, went very well and we all learned great tips on effective advising from each other. We learned best practices. Practices that each of us had been using, sometimes for many years, while the professor next door struggled at the same task and had no idea of the effective practice his or her neighbor was employing.

I see this happening routinely in schools. There seems to be an implicit devaluing of the brain power of educators underlying this plague. While I am on the subject of post-secondary education, I will mention another pet peeve that represents the same wasteful and disrespectful mindset. Most universities, certainly the larger comprehensive ones, have quite a wide range of expertise in the faculty. There are departments of engineering, and architecture, and accounting, and marketing, and education, etc. Yet when a university wants to solve a problem or begin a new endeavor, they hire a marketing firm, or an architect, or an auditing company. Rarely to do they turn to the faculty in their own institution who very well may have educated and trained those outside consultants. I was always a bit miffed that a university is in the business largely of educating adolescents and young adults, and I am an expert in adolescent and young adult development and in education, and no one ever asks me for advice on how the university could do its central function better. But enough about my personal issues.

Schools simply need to do more systematic and intentional sharing to keep best practices from going down the drain, and they need to rely on their staff as a resource for broad-scale organizational quality control and improvement. It is such a waste of a valuable resource to not do so.

Wasting Students' Brainpower

The other brain drain has to do with students. Students have brains too. Even very young students have brains. Their brains may not weigh quite as much as the ones in our big heads, but they are pretty powerful nonetheless. And we are consistently wasting them.

Teachers tend to think of themselves as the sole problem-solvers and decision-makers in the classroom. After all, they are the only ones in their classrooms who have official university degrees in education and who collect a paycheck for educating. By now you may be tired of my harping about the disempowerment of students, about the oppressive hierarchical structure of schools, and about the need to democratize schools and classrooms. Well if you are, buckle your seat belt because here comes more of the same.

Oftentimes students have better ideas and solutions than we adults do. They often see things we miss. Know things we don't know. Or are simply less set in their ways and therefore more, as Margaret Wheatley states it, "open to possibility." And yet we still their voices, or at least dismiss or discount their ideas, and hence waste their brains. This is another foolish and wasteful brain drain. Plus it is utterly inefficient and, if teachers really thought about it, re-capturing the power of students' brains would make their work much easier in most cases.

One of my favorite, and simplest, strategies for harnessing kid power is "ask three, then me." Many teachers do this in various forms and under various names. For example, a teacher will establish a classroom practice that students may not ask a teacher a procedural question about instructions already delivered to the class (e.g., "are we supposed to hand these in?") until he or she has asked at least three other students and still not received the answer. You know the scenario:

Teacher: Take out your social studies book and turn to page seven, and do the odd numbered questions only. Use pencil and I will not be collecting them this time.

Student A: Which page?

Student B: Did you say to do all the questions?

Student C: Are we supposed to do these in pen or pencil?

Student D: Are you going to collect these?

Etc. Etc.

Pretty typical, actually. With the "ask three then me" rule, these questions are still asked, but they are asked of peers, thus freeing the teacher from answering the same annoying questions over and over. It is an efficiency increaser and climate enhancer. But there is more to this than simply aborting the line-up of questioners after such instructions are given. It also structurally promotes student inter-dependence. Students are learning to think of each other as resources, to be resources to peers, and to discover that they don't need authority figures to answer all questions. In Chapter 18, we will return to the fact that underlying these two strategies (only teachers can answer such questions vs. students must ask each other such questions) actually reflects some often unrecognized but powerful theories of schooling, students, teaching, and classrooms, theories that need to see the light of day and be reflected upon. These are examples of the theory in action we discussed earlier.

Another example of the brain drain is problem-solving. In the typical classroom, teachers take the primary responsibility for problem-solving. Sometimes they do a great job of it; other times they don't. And often students could do just as good a job. At other times, they could do an even better job than the teacher at solving a particular problem. I like to tell teachers that empowering students to contribute to problem-solving will allow them to off-load part of their job on the kids and they still will collect their full pay check! What a great deal, eh?

At Francis Howell Middle School in St. Charles Missouri, a social problem arose when students, just before going on a field trip, decided to alter the names on the bus assignment lists so they could sit next to their friends. They had been allowed to sign up themselves for buses, but not everyone had done so in time to be with their best friends, so they erased the names of kids who had signed up and replaced them with their own. Teachers discovered this and were about to scrap the student lists and replace them with teacher-assigned lists, or even cancel the trip. The principal, Amy Johnston, caught wind of this and told the students that they needed to find a solution quickly. They met in small groups, discussed the problem, and created a fair solution of bus assignment. According to Amy Johnston, "the kids who did the erasing were honest and were not allowed to 'get their way' and ride the bus of their choice, but understood why."

It is the open fair discussion aimed at a just solution that leads to such understanding and ultimately acceptance. In acknowledgement of the peaceful, fair, and student-generated resolution, students were allowed to ride the bus of their choice on the way home. This was not a social engineering problem of cataclysmic proportions, but to those young middle school kids, it was very significant. And by allowing the students to solve the problem, there was buy-in to the new plan and no resentment of perceived adult dominance and arbitrariness.

At a Rockwood Summit High School in Missouri, a few students created an un-authorized newspaper and one edition had heavily offensive racist language and ideas. As you can imagine, this caused quite a stir which eventually got into the local news. There was huge tension between racial groups, and the community wanted a resolution.

The principal, Susan Springmeyer, wisely looked for counsel, and then decided, after consultation with me and with staff at Teaching Tolerance, rather than simply ruling by decree, to convene a meeting of the offending students with representatives of the offended (and very angry) student groups. She put them in a circle and told them to work it out. This was a remarkably courageous thing to do and one most school leaders would never dare: to put a group of angry minority students together with three racist journalist students who had offended them and let them use discourse to resolve the problem. But she did and they did. The "journalists" agreed to let representatives of the offended groups preview all future issues of their newspaper to give feedback on what might be offensive. Ultimately they stopped publishing the newspaper entirely, when they realized their sole purpose had been to have an audience for their efforts to put others down.

A second grade teacher, who was in my graduate seminar on character education, came in one Tuesday evening for our meeting and asked if she could use the seminar to help her solve a seemingly insoluble problem. Apparently, the boys in her class had been stuffing paper towels in the sinks and toilets and intentionally flooding the boys' room floor. Apparently this happens more frequently in boys' rooms in elementary, middle and high schools; Freud would likely have had fun explaining this one!. She said, "I've tried everything!" Realizing that she had probably tried a lot, but clearly had not tried "everything," I asked her what she had actually tried. "First I made a rule that there would be a designated restroom time. Then I made a rule that only one boy could go to the restroom at a time. Then I made a rule..."

Well, you get the picture. So I asked her "when did you come into sole ownership of the problem?" She didn't understand what I was getting at, so I further asked, "Do you contribute to the problem? Are you personally impacted by the problem?" Both answers were negative, so I asked, "Then why are you the only one trying to solve the problem?" She was still at a loss, so the seminar members suggested she convene her class in a circle the next morning and announce that "*We* have a problem" and then allow a class meeting to suggest solutions.

At the next meeting of my course a week later, she literally walked in the door and exclaimed, "It's a miracle!" Apparently she had followed our suggestion, and it had worked beautifully. The students had discussed the problem, generated numerous possible solutions, settled on student-elected bathroom monitors, and then enacted the solution. End of problem. My assumption is that if the teacher had dictated the very same solution, it would not have worked.

Kristen Pelster, the principal of Ridgewood Middle School in Arnold, Missouri, a well-deserved National School of Character, was approached a while back by some students who announced, "We have a problem with cheating," to which she replied, "We do?" So she went to her teachers and told them what the students had said, to which they replied, "I don't think so." But Ridgewood is not your typical school and there is little brain drain there. So rather than discounting the students' assessment, given that the administration and teachers disagreed, she decided to act on this. But whereas most administrators would then design an academic integrity program, she simply went back to the students and said, "I don't think we have a cheating problem and neither do the teachers. But we believe you. So what are you going to do about it?" And she simply "awarded" them the problem and enlisted their brains to solve it. They created a new academic integrity program. Interestingly, Don McCabe, who is the preeminent researcher on academic integrity programs, has found that such initiatives are much more effective when they are authentically student-led (for a great resource on this topic, see the Center for Academic Integrity at Clemson University—www. academicintegrity.org—which has much of Don's research plus other helpful information and materials).

I also love invoking the voices of students toward school and classroom improvement. So often when I do this, teachers voice astonishment both at (1) how rich students' ideas are and (2) at the mere fact that students think so deeply about school. The fact that teachers are surprised that students think so deeply about school in turn astonishes me. As we have already established, students are akin to an oppressed class or even prisoners. They spend around 150 days a year, frequently against their wishes, ensnared in your educational clutches. Of course, they think deeply about it. Didn't you when you were a student?

Certainly there are some domains in the school where students are unlikely to be powerful resources, but such domains are far fewer than most adults would expect. And, of course, there are developmental limits on this, so that younger students can contribute less to school planning, problem-solving, innovation, etc. But those little ones can likely do a lot more than most adults give them credit for. This is something I have learned over and over from good early childhood educators and primary-grade teachers. In fact, it would serve most educators at higher grades, including high school, well to spend a few days in a pre-school or kindergarten classroom. They would start to understand just how much they have been selling their own students short by seeing how much the little ones can do.

To make schools work better, and to be more effective and efficient, part of what we need to do is waste management. We need to stop pouring teachers' best practices and kids' ingenuity down the drain. In order to do this we need a few things: (1) we need to understand the problem of brain drain in schools; (2) we need to value the ideas of our students and our colleagues; (3) we need to develop a truly collaborative learning culture in classrooms and schools, and (4) we need to enact classroom, school and district-level policies and practices that not only allow for, but actually elicit the sharing of ideas, rather than pouring them down the drain.

Planned Communities

There are lots of ways to think about schools. Schools can be understood as places of learning, mostly for students, although many schools also serve others in the community, such as parents. Schools can be thought of as places of work for those employed to teach, serve, clean, and transport. Schools can be thought of as means of socializing the next generation of citizens. They can be resource centers for those that live in the neighborhood. They can be thought of as means of brain-washing. They can be seen as the hope for our future or as a great waste of time and resources. And on some level all of these are correct.

But it is helpful to think more sociologically about schools. Schools are communities. I am often tempted to call them mini-communities, but that can be very misleading, because it is relative. Surely, schools count as "mini" when compared to states, countries, large corporations, etc. But they are large when compared to families, compared to small to medium workplaces, compared to many faith-based congregations, and the like. And schools can be fairly large, although I am definitely not recommending that.

I recall hearing about a high school in Los Angeles which had over 5000 students (plus all the teachers and other staff), and had to run in shifts. When I visited Taiwan a few years ago, I was told about an elementary school that used to have 10,000 students! More recently in Taiwan, I visited a high school with over 7000 students. These last few are larger than many colleges and universities, and even the towns many of you have come from or currently live in. So, I will call schools communities and drop the "mini" prefix.

Defining Community

So what is a community? There is no single answer to that one unfortunately. But we can at least identify some core features of a healthy community, that is a community that functions well, serves its members, and has a positive role in the world. First, it is a group of people. I have never met a community of cell-phones or toothbrushes. Second, those people have some common commitment. That commitment may be to a theological system of beliefs, to a shared activity or interest, to a philosophy, or just to each other as a group. Or to a more than one of these. Third, because of the shared commitment, there is a shared identity. The community can be defined and named. And people identify themselves as connected to that name. Fourth, there is an identifiable set of expectations (norms) for how to act and interact. Ideally, these norms are more than lip-service; they are authentic expectations of community functioning. They are reinforced and enforced by community members. And if this is an ethical community, as opposed to an anti-social or destructive community, then the norms must be ethical, pro-social norms. Fifth, there ideally is an emotional attachment both to the community as a whole and to its fellow members. Members care about the community. Sixth, there is a shared interest in preserving the community, protecting it, and supporting and protecting each other as members of the community. The community has value to its members. And consequently, the members serve the community in various ways. They give their time, talents, and/or other resources to it. So,

1. a group of people
2. with a shared commitment,
3. and a shared identity,
4. and a shared set of pro-social, ethical norms
5. resulting in an emotional bond to the community and its members
6. that all lead to serving, supporting, and protecting the community and its members.

This is what a school should be...and do.

How to Build Community

When I worked in Lawrence Kohlberg's Just Community Schools (see *Lawrence Kohlberg's Approach to Moral Education*), a primary focus was on building a shared sense of community based on fairness among the students and staff. That view of a school, where we have an explicit shared identity, collective norms, and an emotional bond to each other and the community as a whole, can be the foundation for a truly great school. By great, I mean a school that both fosters the development of character and citizenship as well as promoting deep and sustainable learning and academic flourishing. In other words, this serves the core purposes of schools that were introduced in Chapter 1.

The problem is that this is not a simple concept to grasp. It is difficult enough in abstraction, but it gets even more challenging when one attempts to apply it through intentional practices and policies and structures. Hence, few educators have such a vision of a school, and far fewer actually attempt to realize such a vision when they recognize it. And even fewer actually succeed in desiring, identifying, and applying effective community-building practices. But it is not impossible. I see it happen every day. And I know many educators who think this way and work to transform their schools into caring communities.

In fact, many of the effective character education and social-emotional learning models that exist use such language in their names: for example, Caring School Community, Communities of Caring, Caring Communities, Ethical Learning Community, Just Community Schools. One of the more interesting trends I have seen in character education, service learning, and social-emotional learning is in fact the ripening recognition that school culture, community, or climate are sociological necessities for promoting healthy development and academic flourishing. John Dewey knew this long ago during the pre-WWII progressive education movement. Kohlberg knew this in the second half of the 20th century as he crafted the Just Community School model. But many others were slower getting on board.

Fortunately, now many recognize that we cannot reach the goals of enduring, sustainable character development and meaningful academic success if we take a molecular look at curriculum, pedagogy, teacher training, reward and recognition systems, and the like. We have to also take a macro-perspective on school as a culture, as a community. In a sense, this is what Philip Jackson meant when he talked about the "hidden curriculum" of a school in his book *The Moral Life of Schools*.

It is also important to note that the development of community in schools is not limited to a whole-school perspective. It also applies to smaller units within the school. Certainly, the same arguments and processes apply to the classroom, especially in elementary schools. They also apply to other subgroups, such as grade levels or the adult community within a school, and to specific organizational groupings like middle school academic teams. But for simplicity's sake, I will mostly discuss this as a whole school phenomenon.

> The strategic plan to build a caring learning community needs two main parts. Part one consists of the steps to take to build community. Part two, and clearly related to part one, is the focus on positive relationships.

How to Build a Caring Ethical Community in a School

How, concretely, can such a community be created? Certainly, the first step is to have a leader or leadership group that can articulate and advocate for movement in this direction. Someone has to convene the community, draft the strategy, and generally shepherd the shift. People have to want to re-think their schools, They also have to work toward significant change, which can be very frightening to many people, in part because the new is unknown and in part because it connotes a condemnation of the status quo. Organizational reform usually begins with a select few visionaries, and it is best if at least some of them are in positions of organizational influence, such as the principal. They articulate the vision and lead the crafting of a strategic plan aligned with that vision.

The strategic plan to build a caring learning community needs two main parts. Part one consists of the steps to take to build community. Part two, and clearly related to part one, is the focus on positive relationships. Remember, we don't want school communities where people just bond to the school, but where they also bond to each other. The importance of building relationships among all members of the community has already been discussed and plenty of suggestions about ways to do this have been presented. So, the focus here instead will be on the first part of the plan, namely, steps to building a sense of community.

Building the Community

Once someone is leading the charge, there needs to be a shift toward collaborative modes of working. Decisions need to be made together. This should be a systematic and pervasive "style" in the school. As was noted in Chapter 10, one aspect of the method behind this seeming madness is that people care more about things they own or create. When we have a voice in making a decision, we are more likely to support and protect that decision, largely because we understand the reasons behind it and because we feel co-owners or co-authors of the decision. Teachers, students, parents, and support staff will also connect to school more if they feel they have an authentic voice in guiding and shaping the school. Another part of the method behind the madness is simply that to become a community one needs to act communally. The act of engaging in shared planning and decision-making about *becoming* a community is already *being* a community.

In my Leadership Academy in Character Education, where groups of school administrators spend a year exploring character education-based school reform, they are asked to do monthly guided reflections and submit their reflections in written form. The first assignment is to create a school leadership team for the character education initiative. They are asked to have that team collaborate on every subsequent reflection and written assignment. This is our sneaky way of getting the participants to put their often authoritarian toes in the collaborative waters. We want to lure them into collaborative leadership. Our hope, of course, is that they will come to see the power and benefits of operating in a more collaborative and communal fashion.

One of the most important collaborative steps is to discover or create a shared identity, set of values, and/or collective norms. What does this school stand for? What is its core identity? What do we expect from members of this community? This can be done through a community forum or retreat.

Suzanne Christopher, an exemplary principal and educational trainer, and I were asked to lead a retreat for the faculty of Floresville (TX) High School so they could create a staff compact about what they committed to do for their students, a process that ultimately won them national recognition from the Character Education Partnership. Or it can be an ongoing process that lasts for months or even years. Or a representative group can be charged to create options that the community reflects upon and chooses between.

In Kohlberg's Just Community Schools, collective norms evolved slowly and, at times, organically in response to real life issues that arose in the school. For example, when one student's money was stolen during school, the entire community met and discussed how this reflected their culture and values. Norms for collective responsibility and restitution, along with property right norms were developed. Discourse and reflection are critical to uncovering and shaping such identity and norms.

Having such values and norms is one thing. Protecting them is quite another. Clark Power (co-author of *Lawrence Kohlberg's Approach to Moral Education*), in studying the Just Community Schools, discovered that norms develop in steps. At first a few leading people advocate for a norm, then most people accept the norm, but only later do people actually expect adherence to the norm from all community members, and that still does not guarantee that people will enforce the shared norm. That is the final step.

So, in the stealing case, at first a few leaders would argue that violating each others' property rights is not reflective of the kind of community they want to be. Such advocacy would eventually (hopefully) lead to the majority (ideally all) of the community members agreeing to this idea. But they may still think it naïve to believe that people would actually change their behavior and adhere to this property norm. If the norm develops further, members perceive wide acceptance and expect to see adherence, and are genuinely surprised at violations of the norm. They may still, however, be unwilling to confront someone who violates the norm. They will be disappointed but still unwilling to enforce it. The norm is fully developed when students, for example, spontaneously stop an act of theft or are willing to report a thief. Excellent schools often report students respectfully confronting other students with statements like, "That is not the Roosevelt Way," or simply, "We don't do that here."

(Intentionally nurturing the development of positive productive cultures in schools has gotten a lot of attention lately, as we have noted before. Two helpful resources are the National School Climate Center, www.schoolclimate.org, and the Building Community Institute, www.cliftontaulbert.com.)

Karen Smith has recounted an incident from when she was the principal at Clearview Elementary School in Washington Missouri. A fifth-grade boy, who had transferred recently to her school, barged into her office and threw himself on the coach, exclaiming "What's wrong with the kids here?" Despite her shock, she asked him what he meant. His reply was, "They won't fight!" Apparently, he figured that he could establish himself in the social pecking order of the student culture by getting in fights and winning them. Whenever he tried, however, the students would not fight with him and many would explain, "We don't do that here." The culture of this school community was so surprising and unfathomable to him that he thought he had landed on an alien planet!

Part of the process of building community comes from having some shared and clear way of representing the identity of the community. Charles Elbot and David Fulton, in their book *Building an Intentional School Culture*, describe a process for creating what they refer to as a "touchstone." All schools have a mission statement, but they are written in the third person ("Main School prepares students for the 21st century...") and typically are too verbose, abstract, and complex to remember fully or be useful in communication. By contrast, the touchstone is a set of easier-to-remember "we" statements that express the commitment of school members to live by the school's core values.

I like to think of a touchstone as a doorway or window into a more complex conceptualization of a school's mission. Elbot's award-winning school (Slavens School in the Denver Public Schools) created a code of conduct that centered on the notion of "taking the high road" as their touchstone:

> **At Slavens we take the high road.**
>
> **We genuinely care about ourselves, each other, and our school.**
>
> **We show and receive respect by: using kind words and actions, listening thoughtfully, standing up for ourselves and others, and taking responsibility for our own behavior and learning.**
>
> **This is who we are even when no one is watching!**

It includes details about what it means to "take the high road." This served as their touchstone and it was widely disseminated, most notably on magnets that staff and family members could post in prominent places.

All stakeholders learned the code of conduct, but it was still quite a mouthful. So spontaneously, a briefer version emerged: "We take the high road," or simply "the high road," served as the shorter informal touchstone. That could easily be put on t-shirts, letterhead, or, more importantly, invoked quickly in discipline conversations. And it was a simple and easy way to call to mind the longer and more complex concepts of the Code of Conduct, the full touchstone.

Students know the concepts underlying the longer mission or, in the Slavens case, the Code of Conduct, and simply mentioning the touchstone would focus their attention on those critical concepts. Once students said and thought about "taking the high road," they were immediately connected to the rest of the Code of Conduct. Kind of like flipping a light switch in a dark room. That simple act makes all the rest of what is in the room easier to see and use.

It is important to note that the Slavens Code of Conduct was created over a full school year by teachers, parents, and administration and through meetings and book studies. Elbot and Fulton emphasize that in order to be effective, the touchstone must be developed with adequate opportunities for input from staff, students, and parents. Schools that have created their touchstones too quickly, without a well-thought-out school-wide participatory process, have found that their touchstone statement ends up being just "words on the wall," with little influence on character and conduct.

If we go back to our six-part definition of community, we can see how a focus on relationships and collaboratively formed values and norms will help a school to become a group of people with a shared identity. Such a school has a conceptual and emotional commitment to the community itself and to its members and beliefs, even to the point of protecting and enforcing the community's norms when individuals do not honor them. But to get to that point, a school has to first recognize the importance of community and commit to it, and then be strategic and intentional in creating a true ethical caring learning community. No task is more important—or ultimately rewarding—in the life of a school.

What Happens Next

We often forget that life does not have a script. We don't actually know what will happen next. Oh, sure, sometimes what happens next is pretty predictable. We have been through the same situation before and we can pretty well guess what someone will say when we say "thank you" or what will happen when we ring our friend's door bell or that the teacher will collect our assignments at the end of the class period, as she does each class period. But we don't *know*. Perhaps our "thank you" will engender a "What did you say?" this time. Or the door bell will short out with a pop and some smoke. Or the teacher will forget to collect the assignments. So even in familiar situations we are dealing with probabilities and guesses. Not with certainties.

For 15 years I was a founding member and performer with an improvisational comedy group in Milwaukee, called "ComedySportz." People came and paid to see us improvise scenes. And they marveled at our unique talent. Improvisation. They watched us stand on stage to be told by the audience that we were to portray amoebas inside Phyllis Diller's upper lip that had just discovered the secret to life. And off we went to improvise that improbable circumstance. We would be those amoebas and have a conversation about life and plastic surgery and comedy and Phyllis Diller. The audience would laugh and then afterwards regale us with adoration for our unique skill. They would talk to us after the show about the show and assure us that they could never do what we do; that is, they were sure they could never improvise.

What they didn't know was that, in the mere act of telling us this, they were actually doing just what they claimed they could not do. My best friend, and the leader of our improvisational show, Dick Chudnow, once pointed out to me that every conversation we had in our lives was an act of improvisation.

Think of any conversation you have had. You didn't have a script, did you? You didn't know in advance what your next "line" would be, did you?

This point is so obvious once you hear it, but I had never even considered the notion previously. None of us has a script for what we are to say when we talk to someone else (other than telemarketers of course, but we all know that their DNA is a bit different than most of the rest of us). So while those audience members were telling us they couldn't improvise, they were in fact at that very moment, by the act of conversing, doing just what they were claiming not to be able to do. It is not much different from when my son, who as a four-year-old and fascinated with construction sites which he called "'struction sites," said, "Dad, do you know why I call them 'struction' sites?" When I said I didn't know, he explained, "Because I can't say 'construction.'"

Scott Jones, a high school social studies teacher at Hazelwood West High School in St. Louis, told me that in his first year of teaching he ran out of content knowledge about history before the first semester had even ended. Impressively, he went back to school to earn a Masters degree in history in order to stock his larder of content knowledge. But we all run out of knowledge or ideas frequently when teaching. I remember my first class (Psychology 101). I was barely out of college, and here I was (as a graduate student teaching undergraduates who were my peers merely four months earlier) in front of a classroom full of students who thought of me as an expert and a font of knowledge. I often found myself painted into a knowledge corner either by my own pedagogical ineptitude or the intelligent and unforeseen questions of my students. So I would wing it.

Now, I am not suggesting teachers make up facts. In fact, a great teaching strategy is to "fess up." It is a great idea to admit that you don't know something and then find it out and report on it another day. It models a true learning ethic, demonstrates honesty, and builds positive relationships with students. But we have to improvise nonetheless. We have to at least say what we do know that is relevant to the perplexing question, and then conjure up and suggest ways to fill in the knowledge gaps. We didn't plan any of this in advance, because we did not anticipate the questions. So we are improvising—although in almost all cases, teachers who do this are not aware that they are improvising.

Components of Effective Improvisation

Effective improvisation takes a few skills. The first is simply the confidence that one can survive improvisation. I know this sounds strange, but I remember the first time I did improvisation in front of an audience. I entered the stage with a deep sense of dread (stage fright). The dread came from a vague but ominous sense that if I failed somehow something awful would ensue. I did not know what it would be but it certainly emotionally felt as if it would cause great harm or suffering at the very least, and perhaps end the universe as we know it.

Of course, the show went fine, I did fine, people laughed, and I discovered that the dark and evil unknown was not a likely result of making things up in front of others. Improvising neither hurt, nor led to disaster. Similarly, I think teachers need to discover that improvisation (and the inherent unpredictability of it) is not dangerous. They must learn not to fear venturing into the untamed and unknowable wilderness of unscripted teaching.

The second skill that a teacher needs is the ability to multi-task. In a classroom, improvisation often is necessitated when one is already engaged in another endeavor (e.g., delivering a lesson). When I was doing my dissertation research, I learned to listen to someone else, write their comments down, formulate a follow-up question, and ask the next question nearly simultaneously. I managed somehow to compartmentalize all these tasks. Similarly, we may have to continue with the lesson as we improvise a variation based on what is happening in the classroom (students don't seem engaged, etc.).

> **Core Competencies of Being an Effective Improviser**
> - Confidence
> - Multi-tasking
> - A playful spirit

One improvisation exercise the ComedySportz players used to do to hone our multi-tasking skills was to sit between two people who were each having a conversation with you, each about a completely different topic. The task was to listen to both simultaneously while shifting back and forth between responding to one or the other appropriately.

Third, you need to be comfortable with play. Improvisation is a form of play. You are playing with reality, playing with ideas, playing with words, etc. You are creating something out of nothing. This should be enjoyable. If it is not, it likely will not be as effective.

Of course, we can also improvise in crises and in serious events. MacGyver (the TV character who kept using his scientific knowledge to fight crime) was known for improvising explosive devices out of a thumbtack, a marshmallow, and an eyelash hair (or something like that). It was serious business. But if it can be joyful, then so much the better (not for blowing things up, that is, but for teaching).

Kids Say and Do the Darndest Things

There is a whole other side to the relevance of improvisation to teaching. Art Linkletter (look him up) made a career out of the unexpected utterances of children: kids say the darndest things! That is not news to anyone who has spent appreciable time with children, such as parents and teachers. And it is not just what kids say; it is also what they do. Kids do the darndest things!

A physician friend of mine told me the story of a mother who came into a community medical clinic with her elementary school-age son. She proceeded to smack him in the waiting room. My friend was quite disturbed by this and demanded to know why she had hit the child. Her reply was an emphatic, "He's an idiot!" Further disturbed by this way of talking about her child, he controlled himself and asked her why she was calling him an idiot. Her explanation: "He ate a rat."

Now my friend was very confused. He asked her, "What do you mean he ate a rat?" She said nothing. She simply opened her purse and pulled out a rat trap with a headless rat still in it. Apparently this young boy found the dead rat in the trap and bit off its head and swallowed it. The doctor remained doubtful that any child would, upon encountering a dead rat in a trap, be motivated to bite off its head. X-rays sadly revealed a rat's skull in this boy's stomach. What would possess a six-year-old child to bite the head off a dead rat is far beyond me. Fortunately, the "darndest" things that most kids do are much less disturbing, but are surprising nonetheless.

Life Happens

And, of course, there are other events that happen in the life of the school that are not precipitated by kids, but are just as unexpected—fire alarms, gas leaks, furnace or air-conditioning failures, power outages, and the like.

Some are minor (a false fire alarm), and some are major (the 9/11/01 terrorist attacks). But the common denominator is that they are unexpected and consequently reactions to them are by definition unprepared, or in other words they must be improvised.

Educators actually have a term for this. It is "teachable moment." However, most educators never realize that the implication of a teachable moment is that they must be improvisational performers. When the unexpected happens, when the teachable moment is to be transformed into a learning experience, the educator must quickly grasp the new reality that has been thrust upon her by the unexpected circumstance and improvise the next moves, whether it is to verbally underscore a point, shift into class discussion mode and facilitate an effective group reflection, or some other relevant learning strategy.

All prepared lessons are not necessarily good lessons. Similarly, all improvised lessons are not necessarily good lessons. One elementary school principal in Kansas was reported to have engaged in what I think is a terrible improvisation in response to one of the unexpected crises I listed above, namely September 11. He already had a tornado drill scheduled that day and decided to continue with it even when the school was, as most schools in the U.S. were that day, in emotional crisis.

Running a drill to prepare for disaster when a real disaster was unfolding seems like emotional overkill to me. But he didn't stop there. Thus far he was following the script. It is when he started improvising that it became really ugly. Not satisfied with one scheduled tornado drill in the morning in the midst of the unfolding of the 9/11 disaster, he improvised a second unscheduled tornado drill for the afternoon! I can't imagine what he was thinking would be the benefit of doing this. It is more like pouring traumatic oil on the flame of a crisis.

Strategies and Resources for Building Improvisational Skills

By now it should be clear that I think good educators need to be--and in reality already are—improvisational performers. But there are levels of competency of improvisation. Beyond the principles I mentioned above (recognition, multi-tasking, and comfort), one can actually hone improvisational skills with training and improvisational exercises. I recommend, for those who live near an improvisational troupe (and there are many around the country, some in much unexpected places), go see their shows. (You can start with the ComedySportz website to see if there is a group in your vicinity: www.comedysportz.com). This is a treat anyhow as most improvisational theater shows are extremely entertaining and often not that expensive. Then find out if they offer workshops (many do) and consider going to one (beware, you may become addicted! I did.).

Also check out your local college or university and see if their theatre department offers classes or workshops in improvisation. Or you can watch improvisation on television (e.g., "Whose line is it anyway?"). I also highly recommend a staff retreat where an improvisational trainer leads the staff through a set of improvisational games (it is a blast). If you don't have someone locally who can do that, read about improvisation and learn some of the game structures (they are akin to party games like "Charades") and play them yourselves. There are many great books on this topic such as Keith Johnstone's *Impro*.

Not only is this fun, it is also a form of team-building when you do it as a staff. And it builds the improvisational skills you need to capture the teachable moments more effectively and to deal with the other unexpected utterances and behaviors of students. Skills like confidence, playfulness, and the ability to multi-task and split your attention. I went to my first improvisation workshop solely to help my teaching. I never expected to perform on stage; that just happened later. But beyond helping with your teaching, it will spill over to many other aspects of your life.

During the years I was performing, we ran many workshops and saw a large assortment of people come through those workshops. Many wanted to be performers (some ultimately did), but some came for different reasons.

One young woman had worked alone on a computer for years and now had been moved to manage a retail department. She was worried about interacting with customers and took the workshop to improve her "people skills." Two others were seriously emotionally challenged and both seemed to improve dramatically while working with us on their improvisation skills. And we were frequently asked to do workshops in business settings to improve corporate culture, reduce stress, build team cohesion, etc.

Teaching is inevitably unpredictable and improvised. First recognizing that and then actively improving one's improvisational skills is a great way to improve schools. I know it helped my teaching (and public speaking).

SchoolSpeak

Teachers talk funny. Consider a form of classroom exchange that is familiar to us all and rarely reflected upon. It is, in fact, the staple of classroom discourse. The teacher will ask the class a question, call on someone who has raised his or her hand, and then evaluate the accuracy of the student's response. It goes something like this:

Teacher: Who knows the names of the ships that brought Christopher Columbus to America? Yes, Rebecca?

Rebecca: One was named *Maria*.

Teacher: Very close. Can anyone help her? Sean?

Sean: I think it was *Santa Maria*.

Teacher: Very good Sean. It was indeed the *Santa Maria*. Now who knows the other two?

Nathan: *Nina*.

Teacher: That's correct, Nathan. So we have the *Santa Maria* and the *Nina*. Can anyone tell us the name of the third ship? Yes, Antonio?

Antonio: I don't remember exactly. Something like *Peter*?

Teacher: You have the first letter right. Can anyone help? Jessie?

Jessie: Like the bean...*Pinto*.

Teacher: Very close. It was *Pinta*. The *Nina*, the *Pinta*, and the *Santa Maria*.

This teacher already knows the answer and is asking the students to demonstrate their knowledge of the same information, and often evaluating the students through their responses. This is common in classrooms, but in the "real world" that exists outside the walls of the classroom it is a pretty unnatural way of conversing.

If you don't believe me, then think whether or not the following has ever happened to you or anyone you know. You are walking down the street, and a friend approaches you:

Friend: Hi.

You: Hi, how are you doing?

Friend: Fine. Say, do you know where the nearest ATM machine is?

You: (thinking for a moment) I think the closest one is around that corner and one block down on the left.

Friend: (enthusiastically) Wrong! There is one just a half-block back that way.

I will wager that you have not had such an encounter. We simply don't talk this way in real life. We typically don't ask each other questions for which we already know the answer. (Unless you happen to be a game show host and I have a deep suspicion that they are not really human.) But in schools we do this all the time. Of course, there is a good reason for this. Teachers need to ascertain what children know, what they are learning, and so on. But it does distort the way students and teachers talk to each other. It produces unnatural discursive mind sets in teachers and in students.

> We need to liberate classroom discourse from the oppressive yokes of unnatural classroom patterns of verbal interaction.

Now, I don't want to suggest either that this form of discourse should be banned, nor that it is seriously harmful. Rather, I simply want to suggest that teachers get in the habit of talking to students in some rather stilted and unnatural ways. What I mostly want to suggest in this chapter is that we need to liberate classroom discourse from the oppressive yokes of unnatural classroom patterns of verbal interaction. We need to help students and teachers learn to have more natural discussions in schools. To just talk like real people engaged in a meaningful conversation. Wouldn't that be novel and nice?

Talking to Kids Is Sometimes Scary

Teachers are not well-trained in and therefore not overly comfortable with promoting natural discourse in classrooms. Of course, some teachers are just natural at having such conversations in the classroom. Other teachers, however, need some help in breaking the bad habit of engaging in a series of dialogic interrogations of their students. And often they are anxious about even having even semi-unstructured discussions with students.

When principal Amy Johnston proposed a once-a-week middle school advisory meeting (typically one adult with about 10–15 students), lasting a whopping 20 minutes, many of the teachers at Francis Howell Middle School became very nervous. One reported having a knot in her stomach all day on what they called Character Connections Class days—a level of anxiety that she said persisted all year the first year. One reason is that Amy decided that there would be no "curriculum" for these meetings. It was up to the teachers to decide what to discuss and how to run the meetings. She understood the importance of genuine discussions with students, and wanted them to be natural. And for some teachers they were. But other teachers did not know how or were to afraid to do that.

I was at Francis Howell Middle School during the third week of the first year of their Character Connection classes, for the express purpose of training both the teachers and the students who were chosen to co-facilitate CC classes in the methods of leading class meetings. When I worked with the students, I did a demonstration class meeting and one topic I posed was simply, "So how is CC going so far?" The answers ranged from great affirmation and enthusiasm to deep complaints. The affirmative reactions focused on how much fun it was to have a class where they could just talk about "stuff." The complaints were things like, "Our teacher doesn't let us talk to each other." "We just do worksheets." "Our teacher won't let us sit in a circle." And the like. The latter comments were likely about the teachers who were uncomfortable just sitting and talking with students, or not comfortable with their facilitation skills for such conversations. Many teachers lobbied for scripted lesson plans. Now about 10 years later, this National School of Character has CC classes *four times a week*, and they are a center point of the school's success.

Conditions for Effective Discussions

One way I have found to be effective in stimulating good discussion among kids is to simply be authentically interested in what they think. If you are really intrigued by their thinking, they will typically sense that and open up. Part of having natural discourse is to create the context in which students know that such discourse is both acceptable and valued. Teachers who are intrigued by what and how students think, rather than merely whether they have learned what we specifically have taught them (looking for the factoids we have tried to shoot into their brains), are more likely to create a natural discursive climate in their classrooms.

> I truly want to know what the students think and am very interested in what they have to say. I don't condescend and I listen closely. I think that is all it takes.

I have had the opportunity numerous times to lead focus group discussions, sometimes with advance planning and sometimes on the spur of the moment, with elementary, middle and high school students. And they are a blast! We get into some great conversations. And in all cases, these are students I have not even met before. A few times teachers have told me that they are amazed at how successful the conversations are and how much the students open up to me. They want to know my secret for getting students to open up and be candid in focus group discussions. I had not even realized that anything special was happening in these conversations, so I had to think about it a bit first. And the first thing I realized is that I truly want to know what the students think and am very interested in what they have to say. I don't condescend and I listen closely. I think that is all it takes.

Another way to stimulate open discussion with students is to intentionally foster a classroom climate that feels safe (most importantly, from the perspective of the students). When students feel emotionally and socially safe in the classroom, again they will be more likely to honestly voice their perspectives. It is not only the teacher's discomfort that can suppress student open discussion, but it is also their fear that something bad (usually ridicule and rejection) will result from taking the chance of saying what they think.

And a core ingredient in such a classroom climate is the collection of relationships from which the community is comprised (see Chapter 13).

A theme that has been repeatedly revisited in this book is the importance of strategically building positive relationships. This is another place where that makes a huge difference. Positive relationships make social interactions feel safer. Classroom discussions are more likely to flourish when students feel safe enough to open up to their peers and teacher.

Strategies for Nurturing Authentic Conversations in the Classroom

• Demonstrate authentic interest in what students think and say.
  —Discuss topics that are important to you and the students.

• Intentionally foster a safe classroom climate.
  —Intentionally nurture positive relationships among all in the class.

• Collaboratively create shared norms for conversations.
  —Discuss and democratically create shared agreements on how we will talk to each other.

Many character education programs and character educators focus on building relationships, especially at the beginning of the school year. *Caring School Communities* (and its predecessor The Child Development Project; www.devstu.org) focuses on "unity builders" at the beginning of the school year. These are activities in which we get to know our classmates and our teacher better and build positive relationships. Hal Urban's book *Lessons from the Classroom* is mostly about what he did in the first three weeks of the high school year to build relationships, establish norms, and develop routines. Most teachers do this naturally, but could do more. And if the problem is not knowing enough of these strategies, well (1) there are books galore describing them and (2) simply regularly share your best practices with your colleagues, as was suggested in Chapter 12 on Brain Drain.

Hal Urban also used the first three weeks of school to establish shared class norms at the high school level. And this is also an important part of Caring School Communities for elementary school students. When students have developed shared agreements about how to treat each other in open discussions (e.g., "What is said here stays here," or "we will listen respectfully to each speaker"), they are more likely to feel safe in opening up in those discussions.

Theodore and Nancy Sizer, in their book *The Students are Watching*, and Parker Palmer, in his book *The Courage to Teach*, all touch on this issue in effective education. Teachers, according to Palmer, need to be authentic. Artificial discourse (such as the teacher-student exchange at the start of this chapter) is far from natural. And all of these authors agree that good education is a conversation. It should be a conversation, they say, between the students, the teacher, and the big ideas at the core of our curricula. Teachers need to authentically facilitate such discussions. Sometimes that is meant figuratively, as when students individually *grapple* (Sizers' term) with ideas. Other times it is meant literally when teachers facilitate students talking to students about the course material.

My son announced one semester in high school that a contemporary issues class was his favorite class. When I asked him why, he replied "Because we just get to sit around and talk about interesting stuff."

Now who thinks this is a good idea?? Anyone?? Anyone??

The Courage to Lead

Keep in mind, much of character education is about school climate (See Chapter 13). The National School Climate Center has anointed school climate as the central concept linking most efforts to promote effective schools and positive youth development (www.schoolclimate.org). The Character Education Partnership (www.character.org) has recently issued a white paper on school climate hightlighting its centrality in character education. The Collaborative for Academic, Social and Emotional Learning (www.casel.org) has given school climate a primary position in its overall model of how to create schools that promote positive student development. And the U.S. Department od Education's Office of Safe and Drug Free Schools has identified national school climate standards as a foundation for how to create safe and drug free schools.

School climate is indeed key. I often think of school climate as analogous to corporate climate. One clear parallel in this regard is the role of the organizational leader. In the corporate world, the CEO is arguably the single most important influence on the corporate culture. Similarly, in education in general and in pursuing the character and citizenship agenda of schools in particular, the school principal is arguably the single most powerful influence on the school climate. (It is important to note that a parallel, indeed identical, argument can be made for superintendents and the climate of school districts.)

In the last chapter, Parker Palmer and his book *The Courage to Teach* was introduced. Well, now that we are turning our scrutiny to school leaders, I want to make a parallel argument about the courage that a principal needs to lead a school and in large part that is the courage to lead culture change in a school.

Sadly, principals often don't realize how important they are or don't want the responsibility to shepherd the climate of their schools. Additionally, many teachers resist the idea that the principal has that much influence. In fact many teachers see the principalship as a revolving door. Recently, in Taiwan, a rule has been established that all principals get a single four-year term and then must change schools (there is the possibility of a second four-year term in the same school, but that is not common). And this has caused concern about the influence of the principal, because all the staff knows he or she will be gone in at most four years.

The Four Ws

Typically, if one spends enough time in schools, one experiences multiple principals, and begins to get jaded about the prospects of any particular principal being an enduring influence on the school, for good or for bad. If they don't like the principal or his or her initiatives, then they may choose to wait them out. For this, Mary Anne Hoppe and I created the "4W model." If the teachers are **W**aiting you out, you have three options: First, work with the **W**illing. Then for the resistors: either **W**in them over or **W**eed them out.

> ### The Four Ws of Dealing with Resistance to New Leadership
> - Many teachers will **W**ait you out, so you have three options:
>   —Work with the **W**illing.
>   —**W**in over the skeptics.
>   —**W**eed out the unsalvageable "bad apples."

Let me use two exemplary schools to illustrate this model, and in particular the last two Ws: winning them over or weeding them out. In 2000, Ridgewood Middle School (Arnold, MO), was a mess. And that is an understatement. Academic success rates in the single digits, low attendance, rampant student misbehavior, community reputation as a horrible school, graffiti and vandalism everywhere, burnt-out teachers who did not like children, etc. The new superintendent, Diana Bourisaw, discovered that she had this problem, and she therefore hired a new principal (Tim Crutchley) and a new assistant principal (Kristen Pelster). They were charged to go into Dodge City and clean it up. Fortunately, they both had graduated from our Leadership Academy in Character Education in St. Louis, and realized that character education principles would serve them well.

They quickly diagnosed the problem as a school that did not care about kids and proceeded to strategically change that. Among all the challenges (parents wanting their kids out of the school, students who misbehaved because they knew no one cared about them, a deteriorating physical plant, ubiquitous graffiti, etc.), they knew the single biggest issue was the teaching staff. Apparently, the school had gotten such a negative reputation that it had long been seen as unredeemable and therefore had become the dumping ground for the unwanted teachers from other schools. Principals had been allowed to dump their bad teachers at Ridgewood for years. If a principal had a teacher who no longer should be teaching students, she could call the district office and get them reassigned to Ridgewood. Hence about two thirds of the Ridgewood staff was comprised of people who should not be teaching, who were bad for students.

So the new leadership team of Crutchley and Pelster crafted a vision, articulated it clearly and passionately, and began helping staff to be the kind of teachers that a good school needs and deserves, including inviting them to join them and help craft and realize the vision.

Then the Ws began. Lots of resistance and lots of Waiting them out. They tried Winning them over. When it became obvious that most of the teachers not only would not support the vision of a school that served student learning and development, but also would never be teachers who were good for students in general, Tim and Kristen had to rely on a more forceful and authoritarian imposition of their shared vision of a good school. They continued to try to Win over the minority of teachers who wanted to do good education, but had to resort, in most cases, to Weeding out the majority of the staff who resisted their efforts. (It looked like a purge was more in order than gentle weeding!)

In February of their first year, Crutchley addressed this predominantly non-compliant and resistant staff and announced that the school was following this path with or without them and if they did not want to fit in, they should think about leaving the school. He felt he had likely overstepped his boundaries, and worried about finding a pink slip on his desk the next morning (assuming that the teachers would call the union or the superintendent to complain). The next day, not only did he still have his job, but about one third of the staff, the Willing, thanked him and promised to support his vision. At the end of the year, however, another one third of the staff left. During the second year the battle continued albeit at a lessened level. After three years, nearly two thirds of the original staff had left. Weeding was complete and had won, as the others were clearly either the Willing or had been Won over. And the new hires, carefully selected to fit the school's new philosophy, joined the bandwagon. Then Tim and Kristen could shift to a more collaborative democratic leadership style, and from there forward the staff crafted together a truly wonderful school.

This bandwagon led to remarkable gains in academic scores (with state recognition for improvement) along with marked improvements in student behavior and attendance. From 2000 to 2010, the school witnessed the following changes:

- The percentage of students meeting state requirements in Communication Arts increased from 30 to 68.
- The percentage of students meeting state requirements in Mathematics increased from seven to 71.
- The average of more than one failing grade per student in each grading period dropped to near zero.
- The number of annual office referrals dropped from 3000 to 300.
- The average daily attendance increased from 89% to over 95%.

The climate became one of collaboration, empowerment, commitment, achievement, and caring. In 2007, Ridgewood Middle School was named a National School of Character by the Character Education Partnership. Of course, they did much more than merely turn over and win over the staff, but that was a critical piece of leadership that made the rest of the initiative possible.

A very different tack was taken by principal Jennifer Reph at Tremont Elementary School in Medford, New York. She was a young and new principal following the retirement of a long-standing and well-liked predecessor. The school was a reasonably healthy school, but the staff did not take to this new young replacement for their recently-departed "mommy." So they acted out and resisted her innovations, particularly her passionate endorsement of language arts reforms. And they were often pretty mean-spirited in their resistance.

But, as they resisted and tried to Wait her out, she chose to focus exclusively on the Win them over approach. She recognized that, unlike the burnt-out teachers at Ridgewood Middle School, they were good teachers around whom she could potentially build a great school. She persisted, survived their pranks, and went into each classroom to teach language arts lessons, when they refused to do so themselves, according to her vision for better instructional practice. It was a lot of work, and the "battle" was draining. But she slowly demonstrated both her commitment/work ethic and the value of the pedagogical approach that she was championing. Ultimately, she Won them all over. Not one teacher left, and in 2005, they were named a National School of Character by the Character Education Partnership.

Whether a leader relies on one or another W—as Jennifer Reph did by Winning them over, or as Tim Crutchley and Kristen Pelster did in using all the W strategies—these approaches are critical for getting past the resistance of staff to the fact or the practices of a new leader. And it clearly takes courage to be that kind of a leader. The principal of a school is often alone at the top, which makes it even more important that courage is part of his or her arsenal of leadership virtues.

The Courage of Leadership

Most good people want to be liked. Leadership often can challenge that goal. As Tim Crutchley, the former principal at Ridgewood Middle School, reports he learned from one of his doctoral professors, once you conclude that a teacher will never become a good teacher and is not healthy for children, then the operative rule should be "never let a bad teacher have a good day in school." This is not easy to do, not pleasant to do, and will certainly engender anger and resentment and dislike in the targeted "bad" teachers. It takes courage for a good person to follow that path.

It also takes courage to be confrontational with teachers, parents, etc. who resist good practices, who do not act in the best interests of children, or who in other ways are holding back the development of a school that optimally serves all members of its community. Having such "courageous conversations" by definition takes courage. Avoidance is much easier, but we must remember that "what we ignore, we endorse." The path of least resistance is also often the path of least value.

Phil Vincent, author of *Restoring School Civility* and president of the Character Development Group, tells the story of a middle school principal he once worked with who, in coming to a new school, discovered he had an unsalvageable "bad apple" as a teacher, and that this teacher's struggles had been going on for a long time and had been well-documented for several years. He tried to get the teacher removed, but the teacher had tenure and the teachers' association protected her. Being both courageous and creative, this principal asked for a meeting with the association president who he valued and liked. During the meeting he talked about the incompetency of this teacher and the association president pointed out that she had rights and did not think there was enough documentation and support to make the case of incompetency.

So the principal informed the association president that from then on all teachers' children in his school (and there were many teachers who lived in this area) would always have this teacher as their math teacher. He also informed the association president that, based on previous experience, it was highly unlikely that these students would pass the algebra entrance exam for eighth grade placement. In other words, while students with other math teachers were learning math, these students would essentially have wasted a year in this incompetent teacher's class. And he then informed the association president that this included his child who would be entering the school next year.

Within a week, with the strong encouragement of the association president (big surprise, eh?), this teacher turned in her retirement papers. Brilliant, creative, and courageous on the principal's part—and perhaps an "ethical aha" moment for the association president.

I also remember an elementary school principal in Wisconsin who noticed that one teacher sent disproportionately more students to the office for discipline than others. To make matters worse, in a highly diverse school the referrals were mostly African-American boys. So her radar went off and she began to investigate.

Her conclusion was that she had a racist teacher on her staff, and she found this totally unacceptable. (By the way, both the teacher in question and the principal were white). After ascertaining that this teacher's racial biases were not going to be changed for the better, she did a number of things (all ethical) to quickly drive this teacher out of the school. She told the teacher how she felt, she strongly urged the teacher to leave, she worked with the district administration to make this happen, etc. This was a hateful teacher who was clearly not going to be transformed into one who would be healthy for all students, and one who needed to find a different profession. Often the system mitigates against being able to remove such harmful adults from schools. Again, this principal's action was courageous and moral.

One of the most dedicated, courageous and innovative educational leaders I have known is Avis Glaze, recently retired Chief Student Achievement Officer and founding CEO of the Literacy and Numeracy Secretariat of the Ontario (Canada) Ministry of Education (and now president of Edu-quest International, www.avisglaze.ca). Before that she was a teacher, counselor, school administrator, and district administrator. In the latter capacity she repeatedly had to be both creative and courageous to either win over skeptics and/or resistors and thwart the underminers. In one case she worked across an entire community to garner broad stakeholder involvement and commitment to a proposed character education initiative. She did this by inviting stakeholders (media, clergy, parents, politicians, etc.) to a series of meetings to identify shared community values that would serve as the focus of the initiative. In doing this, they became co-authors of the initiative and supported the work that many of them resisted at first. Avis was unafraid to take on issues of student dropouts, gay and lesbian students, and racial discrimination, and found respectful ways to communicate with those who disagreed with her, eventually garnering their support or at least their agreement to not undermine her efforts. She found respect and communication to be essential tools in winning them over and sometimes in winnowing them out.

Having the moral courage of one's convictions, along with the ability to socially and emotionally implement such courageous courses of action, are critical to effectively leading a school to excellence. Furthermore, it is a form of modeling good character especially for the adults in the school who also need to act out of moral courage as they both lead their classrooms (or cafeterias or offices) and navigate the morass of varied relationships that surround them every minute of every day.

Characteristics of Great School Leaders

One of the interesting puzzles of life is how frequently we repeat the mistakes of those whose places we take. How often we become our parents in ways we do not want to be (as well as ways we want to) has already been discussed. People often experience the anguish of hearing our parents' words come out of our mouths, as if some unseen inner demon has possessed our souls. Children watch their parents perhaps more intently than they watch anyone else. And experience more behavior by them than perhaps by anyone else. The way they talk and walk is analyzed and criticized as are the way they thought, and certainly the way they treated children...us. So how on earth could we have replicated those loathed mannerisms, annoying figures of speech, emotional chinks, and so on?

The parallel phenomenon for teachers has also been addressed. How many minutes, days, and hours did you spend observing teachers? How intensely and critically did you analyze and evaluate them? So how did you not learn to be the best teacher in the world? It was suggested in Chapter 5 that this may be one reason that teachers so frequently use ineffective, wasteful, and even counter-productive teaching methods, which are simply being replicated from the teachers that taught us or worked along side us.

Well, the same argument can be made for you educational administrators. How many years did you spend under the authority of various principals and assistant principals? If I asked principals to tell me about the best and worst principals they ever served under, they could easily tell me the characteristics of a great principal (and a terrible one). A great principal has a vision that focuses on the best interests first of students and second of all other members of the school community. A great principal has at least above average, if not exemplary, social and emotional skills. He or she has accurate and deep self-knowledge and self-control. He or she has excellent social skills, including the ability to understand others and their feelings, to listen authentically, to build and repair relationships, to mediate conflicts, and to enlist, inspire, and mentor others.

An excellent administrator serves others in the school community, enabling them to do their best work. And is the true instructional leader of the school, knowing and supporting best practices. And of course has the courage to protect the vision and fight for its realization. A great principal has vision, and has the fortitude and wherewithal to shepherd an institution toward that vision. And a great principal understands that it is her responsiblitiy to lead this process, and has the motivation and energy and commitment to do so.

And you could have told me all this because you have seen good examples of this and contrary cases. But do you let this vision guide your practice? What's stopping you? Don't you want to be a great principal?

I often ask principals the following questions: When did you forget? When did you forget what it was like to be a teacher? When did you forget what it was like to be a teacher and work for a lousy principal? To sit through boring staff meetings, or to get ill-informed feedback? And so on. The point—and sometimes it comes across and sometimes it doesn't—is to question why we act in the same ways our former administrators did when we hated that they acted that way.

In Japan, there is a model of goodness that is called "moralogy." It was created by an early 20th century scholar named Chikuro Hiroike. He proposed a method of achieving moral goodness. A

> "Schools are perfectly designed for the results we are getting. If we don't like the results, we need to redesign schools."
>
> —Paul Houston

central part of it was self-examination. He suggested that only through honest self-knowledge could one be a truly good person.

More recently, in their book *Change Leadership*, Tony Wagner and Bob Kegan argue that effective school change must start with the school leader, and that leader must be open to changing himself or herself. Paul Houston, the former executive director of the American Association of School Administrators (in essence the national superintendents' professional organization), once said that "Schools are perfectly designed for the results we are getting. If we don't like the results, we need to redesign schools." As Hiroike and Wagner and Houston would add, this means a willingness and ability to redesign ourselves.

And that takes great courage.

Adult Culture

Now that we have established that (1) the success of a school depends heavily on the school climate, and (2) the school climate depends heavily on the principal of the school, we can take a look at one often over-looked part of this complex system: the adult culture of the school.

When I first starting working with educators and schools to help them figure out how to transform their schools into places where students flourished, not only academically but also in terms of their total development as persons, I started, as I think most do, with a focus on what impacts students' development and learning. So I would teach educators about best practices (as discussed in Chapter 11). I would teach them how to employ character-friendly methods like class meetings, cooperative learning, and service learning. I would help them understand effective class-room management practices such as developmental discipline. And all of this did in fact help many of them in improving their practice and their schools.

> I realized that I had it backwards. Character education doesn't start with students. It ends with students. It starts with the adults in the school.

But, at the same time, I was running the Leadership Academy in Character Education for school leaders (mostly principals and assistant principals), and listening closely to their perspectives and concerns. And the concerns I heard most frequently had little to do with teacher methods. Instead they had to do with teachers themselves.

Chapter 20 includes a discussion of how complex and difficult teaching in general and teaching for character are. Chapter 9 introduced a more sociological perspective in looking at the authoritarian and often oppressive culture of schools. All of this, coupled with my early work with Lawrence Kohlberg on the moral atmosphere of schools, got me to thinking about schools as social systems. And then I realized that I had it backwards. Character education doesn't start with students. It ends with students. It starts with the adults in the school.

It was easy for me to get this wrong, because I am not an educator. I am a developmental psychologist. The reason, as I suggested in the introduction to this book, that I am even interested in education at all is because education has a significant impact on children's and adolescents' development, especially their moral development. So it is natural that I would emphasize and over-accentuate what we do to and for kids in schools. And yes, that is of great importance.

But if one really wants to impact schools and the students they serve, then one has to recognize that the place to start is with the adults in the school. In the preceding chapter, we considered how important the leaders of a school are. That was my first epiphany. I had to work with school leaders first if I ever wanted to significantly impact students in schools. But I assumed that what I needed principals to do was to get their teachers to master and employ the methods I had assumed (and that research supported) would promote the positive development and learning of students.

What I missed was the middle step. Before the principals could get the teachers to join the bandwagon (remember the Win them Over part of the 4W model in the last chapter?), they had to create a positive adult climate in the school. And that is what I want to focus on in this chapter.

The need to begin with teachers became even clearer when I learned from Hal Urban about the most toxic place in a school. Go ahead, ask any school staff that question and they will very likely reply in instantaneous unison "the faculty lounge." I have done this many, many times and only once did a school staff not immediately answer in this way. It is toxic because it is rife with gossip, back-stabbing, and whining and complaining (Hal has a great lesson on this in his book *Lessons from the Classroom*).

But before we tackle this head on, I want to share one more epiphany that I have had on this journey from being an egg-head basic social science researcher to an expert in character education. It took me less time to recognize that before I taught classroom methods to teachers, I had to focus on teaching them to craft a positive social and learning climate in their classrooms. When biologists try to grow a strain of some organism in the laboratory they use the term culture. They "culture" the bacteria. They grow it in a "culture" dish. This is a great metaphor. If teachers are to grow positive character and academic success in their classrooms, then they have to create a culture in which it will thrive. So, first the culture, then the methods. Of course, this is not as clean a distinction as I make it seem. Many methods serve both purposes. But at least conceptually, and often procedurally, this distinction is important.

Well, the rest of this epiphany is that there is a remarkable parallel between the teacher-to-students-within-a-classroom-culture and the principal-to-teachers-within-a-school-culture. Just as I made a strong parallel between the parent-child and teacher-student relationships in Chapter 7, I want to make just as strong a parallel between the teacher-student and principal-staff relationships. So just as the teacher must first create a classroom climate that supports student development and learning, the principal must create an adult culture in the school that supports positive and effective education of students.

At this point in my own learning curve I developed a simple three step model for effective character education:

1. Spend a year with the principal, getting him or her to "get it" and learn how to lead the development of a school of character (which is precisely what I do in our year-long Leadership Academy in Character Education).

2. Support the principal in Year Two in creating a positive adult climate that will be supportive of positive school reform and character education.

3. Only then, in the third year, start implementing practices that directly impact students.

Now, I realize that very few educators will actually do this in a segmented stepwise fashion, but as a conceptual model it helps clarify what should have primacy in this long and difficult journey to excellence. Most of the great principals I know, and many have been cited in this book, either figured this out themselves or heard me say it and took it to heart. I will give a few examples as we move through this chapter. But first I want to describe one school where this worked well for me and for them.

> ### Three Stages of Comprehensive Character Education
> 1. Leadership development: The leader learns what character education is.
> 2. Staff culture: The leader nurtures a positive ethical staff culture.
> 3. Student character education: The school intentionally implements comprehensive character education.

Taking Time to Put the Adult Culture First

At Brentwood Middle School in Brentwood MO, the principal (Julie Sperry) and her then assistant principal (Eileen Roberts) both graduated from our Leadership Academy in Character Education. This is a very small middle school in a geographically small community with two small elementary schools and one small middle school and one small high school. One of the elementary schools, Mark Twain, has been described earlier in this book as a simply superb school with a master principal, Karen Smith. Julie and Eileen were fervent about character education and were enthusiastically leading the charge for their school to follow in the National School of Character and Blue Ribbon School paths that Mark Twain had successfully traveled.

The problem is that they were leading the charge and no one was following. The teachers were not buying in. In fact, they were pushing back. After about two years of such a tug of war and frustration, I called a "time out." Here is what I told Julie: "I want you to stop doing character education."

When she looked confused, I continued: "Beginning at the start of next year, no more character education. Instead I want you to do two things. First, I want you to build a personal relationship with each teacher. Get to know them, let them get to know you, and spend time having fun with each of them." This was a small school with a small staff and that made it easier to do this. "Second, I want you to go up to each teacher, say the following, and mean it. 'What can I do to help you be the best teacher you can be?'" You may recognize this as a way to do what I suggested in Chapter 11; that is, school leaders working every day to bring each teacher closer to the kind of teacher we all want in our classrooms.

The suggestion I made to ask each teacher how you can help him or her become a better teacher is something even more that it appears on the surface. It is *servant leadership*. I am a member of the Greenleaf Center (www.greenleaf.org), which is the national organization for servant leadership and the reason I belong is because I think it is one of the most powerful models for leadership around. To quote Robert Greenleaf, who founded the servant leadership movement, "*the great leader is seen as servant first*, and that simple fact is the key to his greatness." And that those who follow a leader "*will freely respond only to individuals who are chosen as leaders because they are proven and trusted as servants.*"

In essence, what I asked Julie Sperry to do as the leader of Brentwood Middle School was to be a servant leader. And in that way, others would be more likely to follow. Recently Julie reported that she had indeed followed my advice and that her school had turned the corner, and in fact has just been honored as a 2012 National School of Character, based in part on their recent marked gains in academic achievement and student behavior.

In Chapter 4, I described how I startle educators into an epiphany about having to be a model of character by asking them, "How dare you ask a child to be something that you either can't or won't be yourself?"

Well, it applies here too. How dare we try to create classroom climates that we are unable or unwilling to create among the adults in the school? We need to clean up our own houses before we clean up the climates in our classrooms.

Remember the paraphrase of Gandhi to "be the character we want to see in our students"? Well, we also must have the culture among the staff that we want to see in our classrooms.

It Starts with Leadership

When working with school leaders, it is important to get them to see that it is part of their job descriptions to engineer this adult culture change. Sadly, just as I have noted that in both teacher preparation and in-service professional development we are failing to adequately address classroom management, and more so the skills that teachers need to shepherd a positive classroom climate, so are we failing in administrator preparation to enlighten and equip administrators to focus on and effectively shepherd the adult culture of a school. In other words, they don't know they are supposed to do it and they don't know how to do it.

Just as we ask teachers to invest in the first few days or even weeks of the school year to strategically and intentionally nurture the development of positive relationships among all members of the class (student to student, student to teacher), I ask administrators to strategically and intentionally foster the development of positive relationships among all adult members of the school community. This includes administrator relationships with teachers, of course. But it also includes teacher-to-teacher relationships, teacher to support staff, etc. And yes, it is the principal's job to tackle this. In fact it may be the principal's most important job.

A few years ago, I presented a full day workshop in an elementary school. As the closing of a long and productive day, I decided to just do a fun "unity builder" among the teachers to end the day on a positive, albeit frivolous, note. The staff was to simply mill around and gently greet each by name and shake hands. As I was describing the activity, one teacher sidled up to me and seeming uncomfortable whispered in my ear that the staff could not do this activity. I was confused. Was there an outbreak of leprosy in the school? Was there a religious cult here that believed there was dark power in invoking another person's name? So I asked.

The answer was that they did not all know each others' names. Now this was a large elementary school with about 1000 students and 60 teachers. But that is not SO large that they couldn't all know each other and their names. Oh, and did I mention that this workshop was being run in May, at the end of the school year? That's right, at the end of a school year in an elementary school, and the teachers did not know each others' names.

My first thought was that this was a failure of leadership. The principal had clearly not prioritized a positive adult climate in this school. Or else he would have made sure that at the beginning of the year the teachers all got to get to know one another—well.

Strategies for Building a Positive Adult Culture

How does one do this? There are lots of ways. So I will only mention a few. Introductions and unity building activities in faculty meetings serve the same purpose as the unity builders that teachers do in classrooms. Get to know each other and have fun experiences with each other. Be silly, laugh, and learn about each other in such activities.

Engage in activities where you learn about each other. I run a week-long summer institute in character education and focus heavily on trying to build a community among the 30 or so educators who come to this workshop. So we do lots of unity builders.

One of the more intensive ones I learned from colleagues in Kansas City in the Basic School Center. In this activity, each person draws his or her own life line indicating peaks and valleys in their lives thus far. Here are the exact instructions in case you'd like to do it:

1. Each person is given a large piece of poster paper and access to assorted colored markers.

2. They are asked to take time to draw their own lifeline (about 30 minutes). It must graphically show the course of their lives (at least up to the present, but future speculation is allowed), especially indicating high and low points. They must annotate to name those peaks and valleys.

3. There are no requirements or instructions on the format of the time line, so they tend to vary a lot.

4. Assign participants into groups of three. Do this before they finish their time lines. Ideally they should be heterogeneous groups and people who do not know each other, either at all or well.

5. When all three members of a group are done, ask them to assemble in a quiet place and give them a pad of small post-it adhesive notes (around one inch by one inch or slightly larger).

6. Instruct them to take turns presenting. One person presents his or her life line and the other two are "analysts." They are instructed to look for evidence of character strengths in the presenter's narrative and to jot down a word or phrase characterizing that strength on a separate

post-it for each observation. They are not allowed to speak during the presentation. When the presenter is done, each of the "analysts" takes a turn explaining each post-it/strength and then placing it on the time line on the corresponding place where it was manifested.

7. This procedure is then repeated for the other two members so everyone gets a turn presenting his or her life line and receiving affirmative feedback.

The first time I saw this was at a workshop in Kansas City for two elementary schools. There was a middle-aged man there who I later learned was a long-time teacher's aide in an urban elementary school. He was an immigrant from South Vietnam. The event that stood out was the revelation that the rest of the staff received about and by him in the process of listening to his autobiographical presentation.

Apparently he was in the South Vietnamese Army during the Vietnam War. He was captured and put in a North Vietnamese prisoner of war camp, where he and his fellow prisoners were held in cages and tortured every day for years. He said that he only stayed alive by focusing on his faith and his belief that he would survive and be reunited with his wife and children and parents someday. Eventually, he and a few other prisoners killed a guard and escaped through the jungle and walked all the way back to South Vietnam with no food and no weapons right through a war zone. And eventually he emigrated to the U.S.

A truly remarkable story. What made it even more remarkable is that apparently, even though this man had worked in the school for many years, no one else in the school had known any of this about him. They were stunned, as was I.

I recall doing a workshop in a middle school and witnessing two teachers who knew each other well and had worked side by side for years discover in a similar activity that they had gone to the same high school in a different state. They never knew that before.

Of course, I have been in many schools where the staff was more like a family. They knew each other and each other's families. They played and socialized together. They celebrated and soothed each other. Those are the great schools and one indicator is that there is little or no staff turnover in those schools. Many years ago I was invited to Fairbrook Elementary School near Dayton, Ohio, to help them move from good to great, which they did eventually earning recognition as a National School of Character. It was an easy move because they had a great principal and a great staff culture already. I think they had only had to hire three teachers in 11 years. It was clear that they were a family.

I was working with half of the staff in the morning and half of the staff in the afternoon while substitute teachers were covering their classes. In the afternoon, one teacher abruptly stood up and said, "I think Meghan needs a hug" and ran out of the room. Apparently Meghan was a student in her fourth grade classroom whose best friend had recently died of cancer. When the teacher returned from delivering her love to Meghan, another teacher stood up and announced, "Hey, what about me? I need a hug too!" which initiated a spontaneous hug-fest among the teachers in the room. I didn't need any other measure of the adult climate in that school.

> Great schools require not only great leaders, but great adult cultures. It is up to the great principals to envision, prioritize, and shepherd great adult cultures.

Along with getting to know each other, positive relationships come from just having fun with each other. How often do we invoke memories of goofy times we have had? We kindly tease each other about them ("I still think you look great as a cheerleader" to the male staff member who dressed as a female cheerleader on a "bet" with the student body). We share pictures of us being goofy together, and we try to replicate such fun times.

And we affirm and give thanks to each other. One nice tradition is the "run for the roses" where someone brings a dozen roses (or to save money a dozen mini-candy bars, etc.). Someone takes one and says, "This is for Janet, for bailing me out when my computer broke and I couldn't fix it." Janet comes up and takes the candy bar or rose. Then someone else runs up to be the next to affirm a peer. And this repeats until all are distributed.

Another key point is that the adult culture includes ALL adults in the school. All too often, support staff and para-professionals are not included. Great schools respect everyone and include everyone. Support staff are included in professional development. Relationships are intentionally nurtured among all adults. A few schools have adopted a strategy I developed where each classroom or advisory "adopts" an adult staff member who does not have a classroom or advisory. They build relationships between the teacher and the adoptee and the students and the adoptee.

Of course, for anything of these to happen, the leader has to advocate it, initiate it, model a style that supports it, etc. But sometimes training is necessary, too.

One elementary school principal in Missouri, upon moving to a very successful and privileged school, discovered a rough spot. The staff, and this is not uncommon, would engage in gossip and back-stabbing rather than directly confronting each other. This principal began to have courageous conversations with them to model it, but also more directly trained them in how to have such conversations with each other. This is not an easy thing to do, but luckily she was both a strong leader and had training and experience in how to teach adults to have such conversations. She reports that it had a huge impact on the school climate.

Students flourish best in great schools. Those places are the petri dishes and media in which students grow and flourish. And great schools require not only great leaders, but great adult cultures. It is up to the great principals to envision, prioritize, and shepherd great adult cultures.

Chapter 18

What on Earth Are You Saying?

In Chapter 4, it was established how your actions speak louder than your words, and therefore it's critical to model the character you want to see in students.

In Chapters 5 and 6, the surprising tendency of educators to implement high-glitz, low-impact strategies that they would never use with their own children was examined.

Chapter 15 took a look at the ways teachers speak that seem so unnatural.

So you may be starting to notice another theme in this book, centering on the messages teachers send, often unintentionally. And that is precisely the focus of this chapter. We all have had the experience of saying something and then wishing we could take it back. The following incident has haunted me my whole life.

As an obnoxious, arrogant adolescent, I frequently liked to make satirical fun of my parents, who were caring and patient and tolerant of my demonic adolescent journey. One evening my parents had some friends and relatives over, and I came barging through the living room, full of my teen angst and hubris. I noted a new set of placemats on the counter, and made some sarcastic comment about us not needing to waste money on yet another set of placemats.

What I didn't know was that my aunt and uncle had brought them as a house gift. I loved my aunt and uncle and also knew they did not have a lot of money. I felt terrible and there was no way to *take back my words*. Wouldn't it be nice if life had a "back space" key? Alas, it doesn't.

And I am one in particular who could really use that because I often speak before I consider what I am saying and what its impact might be. Impulsivity, arrogance, and verbal fluency are a volatile combination as

I have experienced time and again throughout my life (and being a New Yorker puts me at a decided disadvantage in this matter. We tend to be pretty "in your face" and direct).

But what troubles me further is the probably countless times when I have said something imprudent, hurtful, counterproductive, or in other ways unwise *and not known it*. How many others' feelings have I trampled and never known? How much damage have I done and still have no idea it happened or that I caused it?

Ways We Send Messages

Well, I may do it more than most others, but ultimately we all do it. And one of the ways we say things we shouldn't is without words. In our examination of the inevitability and power of modeling (Chapter 4), the discussion touched on what has been said eloquently by Ralph Waldo Emerson: "What you do speaks so loudly that I cannot hear what you say."

Now an interesting sidebar on this is the oft-quoted quantification of the impact of our speech versus our non-verbal messages (intonation, body language, etc.). Daniel and Kenneth Cooper (in their forthcoming book *High Payback Learning*) have debunked the common usage of a couple of heretofore widely accepted "findings." One of these, from Albert Mehrabian, is that what we say accounts for only 7% of the meaning conveyed, whereas how we say it—that is, vocal inflection and facial expressions—accounts for 93%. However, this assertion has more recently been challenged and its validity appears to vary extremely, depending on how such communication is studied.

A similar finding is often referred to as the Learning Pyramid and it claims that after two weeks we remember only 10% of what we read and 20% of what we hear, but 50% of what we see and hear. In fact, there is little research behind this assertion, and it originates in a 70-year-old metaphor of a pyramid that was never meant to be taken as empirical fact. But regardless of what the relative impact of verbal and non-verbal cues is, it is clear that what we say is only part of the message we send.

And the other parts of the impact of what we say varies widely, depending on their context. Some of what we say is certainly in the words we use. Some is in the way we say things, such as in our tone of voice. Saying, "That's a great haircut" with one intonation can be affirming, but saying the same words with a sarcastic tone of voice can be hurtful or inflammatory. And then there is our body language. Rolling one's eyes while making the sarcastic statement gives quite a different meaning than smiling sincerely. Most of us are well aware of these nuances in communication.

Yet another way that teachers communicate is by their choices, practices and policies. How do you respond to violations of classroom rules? Or tardy work? How do you respond to student challenges or suggestions? Do you treat some students systematically differently than you treat others? And so on. What I want to suggest is that you often are "saying" something other than (1) what your words overtly suggest and (2) that you even intend to communicate.

To demonstrate this I want to return to a couple of examples introduced earlier in the book. First, let's revisit the "ask three then me" procedure that many teachers have adopted. This is the procedure whereby students know that they cannot ask a teacher to repeat or explain directions until they have asked three peers and still not gotten the necessary information. So let's compare the messages sent by a teacher who uses the Ask3 procedure and a teacher who more traditionally fields questions from students asking for repetition or clarification of directions that have just been given by the teacher to the class.

The traditional procedure goes something like this:

Teacher: (having finished giving directions) Now are there any questions?

Tommy: Which page did you say?

Teacher: Page 16. Weren't you listening? Andrea why are you whispering?

Andrea: I was asking Celeste which questions you said we should do.

Teacher: Why are you asking Celeste? I just asked if there are any questions. You know you are not supposed to be talking to each other.

You get the picture. Now if we contrast this to the Ask3 class, we would see students whispering around the room, the teacher moving on to another task, and no reprimanding discourse between teacher and students.

And if we consider the message being sent, not by the words themselves, but by the very policy, we would also see quite a difference. The traditional teacher has essentially sent the following messages to the class:

- It is bad for students to talk to each other in this classroom.

- It is undesirable for students to help each other.

- I, the teacher, am the only competent resource in this classroom.

By contrast, the Ask3 teacher has alternatively sent the following messages:

- Cooperation is a value in this classroom

- We are all resources to each other here

- Students talking to students is accepted and encouraged

I am not sure that all teachers even understand these messages when they send them. But the difference is remarkable.

Now let's revisit a second example from Chapter 10. You may remember Linda Rayford, the kindergarten teacher who so deftly and productively handled the two boys (Ray and Peter) who decided to sit in the same seat and neither wanted to budge. She repeatedly made choices that sent developmentally nurturing messages to both of these five-year-olds and their classmates. Simply by acknowledging their circumstance (two boys in one chair with one set of materials for the class project), instructing them to "work it out" and walking away, she sent the message to them and any others listening in that she believed they were competent enough to solve their own problems. Many high school teachers never send this message to their 17-year-old students!

Then when Ray asked Peter to move to another seat and Peter rather begrudgingly begins to comply, Rayford checked with Peter over whether that was okay with him. When he said no, she asked him to sit back down and try to find another solution that worked for both of them. Most teachers would glory in the quick "resolution" and move on. Peter would be resentful (even indignant and morally wounded) and the message would have been that expediency and power prevail here. But instead Rayford sent a message that justice and care are key values in this classroom and all students matter.

Then when a third child (Mike) chimed in and suggested a solution, Rayford not only listened but steered the ensuing exchange to Mike's suggestion and worked hard to be sure both Ray and Peter had understood it. A more typical and less tuned in teacher likely would have instead said, "Mike, why don't you mind your own business!?" or "Mike, don't you have your own work to do?" The message sent would have been, much like the non-Ask3 teacher; that is, that students shouldn't try to be resources or talk to each other in this class. Rayford's message instead is that we are an interdependent community, we all matter, our voices are important, and helping each other is a good thing.

So think about what you really want to say. And then consider what you actually are saying. Not just with your words (but of course with them too), but also with your non-verbal cues and your policies and practices.

You will be astonished at the ways you are sending messages that even run counter to what you value. And this book is largely about how we nurture the values and character of our students. This is another key way in which you do that.

Now, what were you saying?

I Beg to Differ

I am sure that by this point, and likely much earlier, you have disagreed with something in this book. Good. As I stated from the outset, I am a constructivist, and a large part of the impetus for writing this book is the fundamental belief that we grow (develop) partially because we confront ideas and experiences that (1) we do not fully grasp at first blush and/or (2) we judge to be wrong. Neither of these outcomes is bad.

In fact, from a constructivist standpoint they are desirable. As I frequently state in my workshops, if you leave my workshop agreeing with everything I have said, learning nothing new, and essentially unchanged, then we have just wasted our time together.

But what matters, perhaps even more than being unsettled or confused by what we see, read, hear, etc., is what we do with that information or experience and with our confusion or disagreement. Do we suppress it and not think about it anymore? Do we get angry and rail against the "bad" ideas we have heard? Or are we, as Margaret Wheatley suggests, open to the possibility, and, as Ted and Nancy Sizer suggest, do we grapple with making meaning of the disjunction between our previous understandings and that which is unsettling us? I don't think it will be too difficult for you to conclude which path I recommend.

Such grappling is essential for growth. It is part of the dialectic of life. The growth of the person and new ideas develop from the conflict between two seemingly incompatible ideas. How can the earth be round and we don't fall off? How can light be both a wave and a particle? How can an adolescent want his mommy and daddy to be his safety net and want so desperately to be independent of them at the same time? How can human behavior and development be caused both by nature (genetics, biology) and nurture (experience in the world)? Reconciling seemingly incompatible ideas has always led, in the broad sweeps of human understanding and growth, forward.

In examining the purposes of education in the first chapter, it was argued that one of those purposes was socialization of future citizens of our democratic society. And that to be an effective citizen, and to support the flourishing of the democratic system and society, one needs not only knowledge of democracy and government (and they are important) but also to develop the dispositions, skills, and character that support effective productive democratic participation. This includes the motives to be part of the public sphere (the motive to acquire the knowledge necessary for civic literacy, the motive to work to find the best path to supporting the common good, etc.). But it also includes the virtues necessary to effectively contribute to that search for the common good in the public sphere (the patience to listen to others, the care for consensus and the well-being of those with whom we disagree, etc.).

And the willingness and capacity to dissent. Now there are many different perspectives on democracy and citizenship and not all will align with this perspective. But I want to argue that this willingness and capacity for respectful dissent is necessary for the flourishing of our democratic society. And it doesn't come out of thin air. It is either nourished or suppressed. And our hierarchical authoritarian schools are more likely to suppress it than nurture it, just as was so strongly argued in Chapter 9 in drawing a parallel between schools and prisons. Just as the authoritarian and hierarchical organizational structure of prisons is rather unlikely to support and nurture dissent, so is the authoritarian and hierarchical nature of most of our schools. And I think I have made it pretty clear that a fundamental purpose of schools is to foster the development of character of students, both civic and personal character.

Early in my career, when I was mostly doing basic social science research, I focused on peer moral discussion as a means of promoting the development of the capacity to think critically about matters of right and wrong. My colleague, John Gibbs, and I called these discourse skills *transactive discussion*. We studied it and wrote a manual for coding it, and spent endless hours poring over adolescent peer moral dialogues to learn more about its nature and impact.

One of the things we found (as did others who later studied this phenomenon) was that peer moral discussion tended to be intellectually contentious. Not always but very frequently. Discussants would argue strongly for their own positions, aggressively attack their peer's differing position, and staunchly defend their own positions against such attacks. They were not dogmatic and entrenched but their framing perspective was one of "winning" the debate.

But more interestingly, the discussions where there was more of the "thinking about each other's thinking" in dialogue produced the most growth in the participants' moral reasoning capacities. This intellectual tussling fostered moral growth. Whether or not it was good for the soul is beyond my ability to judge, but it was clearly good for the mind and specifically the moral thinking part of the mind. Here's an example of that kind of growth-producing dialogue:

Alena: I don't think it is ever justified to lie.

Kris: Why not?

Alena: Relationships depend on trust. You can't have a relationship if you don't trust someone. If you lie to me, I won't trust you.

Kris: Yeah, but what if telling the truth will kill someone? Like that story with the Nazis coming to ask someone if they know where Jews are hiding? If you tell the truth, they will die.

Alena: Well, I guess that is different.

Kris: Why?

Alena: I don't know. It just seems that you raised the ante here. Now it is a matter of life and death.

Kris: Exactly. I think life trumps honesty.

Alena: I hadn't thought of that. I guess you are right. Generally it is wrong to lie, for exactly the reasons I said. But not always. Not when a life is at stake. Greater good kind of thing.

Kris: Yeah, that was what I thought, too.

Earlier in the book I mentioned a focus group I once ran at Belleville West High School in Illinois. One of the issues that surfaced was student discontent with the district's dress code. Students had little avenue for voicing their discontent until this focus group, so they seized the opportunity to dwell on it a bit. It seems the district school board had crafted the dress code without student input and students found it to be both complex and cumbersome as well as simply difficult to follow.

As they began to describe some of the details of the plan, I started to realize how accurate their assessment was. Variations on when and where you could wear certain types of garments (e.g., hoodies), what colors one could wear (black only if it was a part of athletic wear), what size imprinted school logos could be (varied depending on the type of garment) all led to a dress code more complex than the federal tax code!

To his credit, the principal, Bob Dahm, heard the students' concerns and agreed to form a student dress code committee to consider changes. And to the credits of the students, they made it quite clear that they were not looking to wear provocative or risqué clothing, but simply to have a simple, practical, and appropriate set of rules for attire. Without the opportunity to dissent, the dress code would have remained a problem bubbling below the surface of the school and weakening the climate.

This notion that students often notice that the emperor is wearing no clothes, but have little opportunity to dissent, picks up the themes in Chapter 12 (Brain Drain) that we waste students' brains, Chapter 10 (Hearing Voices) that we do not adequately make space for students' voices in schools, and Chapter 9 (Sentenced to School) that schools are authoritarian, hierarchical and disempowering institutions. If we truly want to foster schools that are democratic, autonomy-supportive, and developmental, then we need to promote and empower productive student dissent.

Recently, Bill Puka (a moral philosopher) and I wrote a paper on "educating for dissent." Our argument was precisely what I have been presenting thus far in this chapter, namely that democracy requires debate and dissent and schools need to take that as part of their charge, as part of the civic purpose of schools as well as the unavoidable character purpose of schools. The founding fathers understood well that the success of this daring experiment in self-governance of the new nation depended on the character of its citizens. And well before that, Heraclitus asserted that "character is destiny." Good people are more likely to make a good world than are bad people.

And part of being a good person is having the knowledge, skills, and dispositions necessary for respectful, reasoned, productive dissent. Just as with character in general, we need to make this a priority and then strategically and intentionally redesign our schools to effectively foster the learning and development that it requires.

So, do you agree? Well it is just fine if you don't—as long as you have good reasons and share them respectfully.

Rocket Science

I get tired of hearing how it really isn't so difficult to educate students. How it really isn't that hard to design and/or run an effective school. That being a teacher or a principal is relatively simple. That the methods and strategies of running schools that turn out well-informed, critically-thinking, socially-sensitive and ethical students "aren't rocket science."

Oh, yeah? Then answer this one: if this stuff is so simple and easy, then why is it so rare? Certainly, there are great schools out there. But they are not the norm. Most are simply good, slightly above average, hitting on most but not all cylinders. Plenty are mediocre, and, sadly, some are just plain bad.

You can take a bad or good school and make it great, but that transformation is rare as well. Sustaining

> Schools have to be constantly renewing "organisms." That alone takes a lot of ingenuity and work.

excellence for more than a few years is a challenge. Jim Collins, in his book *Good to Great*, made the same point quite powerfully and eloquently, in his case about corporate organizational change. It takes a lot to achieve organizational greatness (only a very small minority ever gets there), and it takes a lot to sustain it once you have gotten there.

Just as this applies to corporations, it also applies to schools. In one sense it is even harder in schools because schools are generational institutions. Their key constituencies, students, move into, through, and then out of the school in a cyclical fashion. It is hard to sustain a culture when the great majority is only around for at best a few years. Of course, other institutions face this challenge as well; a good example is the military, many of whose members stay only a few years. Even career military typically rotate through a series of one-, two- or often at best three-year assignments. Likewise, schools have to be constantly renewing "organisms." That alone takes a lot of ingenuity and work.

A great and effective school is a complex and fragile thing. A lot of different variables determine the quality and impact of a school. And these variables combine and interact in a complicated and delicate formula that often fails to work or, if it does work, fails to sustain. The preceding chapters have elaborated many of the ingredients in this formula. At the top of the list is leadership, which itself is multifaceted and can succeed in a number of different guises, or it can fail for lots of different reasons. No healthy school culture is leader-proof; that is, an ill-intended or inept leader can undo any positive school culture. But without committed, enlightened, socially intelligent, and sustained leadership, no school will be great.

> No healthy school culture is leader-proof; that is, an ill-intended or inept leader can undo any positive school culture.

School leaders, as we saw in Chapter 16, wear a variety of hats: they are the visionaries for the school improvement plan, social leaders of the adult and whole school cultures, instructional leaders of the methods needed to provide excellent education, role models who walk the talk and talk the walk, and ambassadors to the parents and broader community for the school's welfare and vision. They need to be sensitive to subtle but powerful influences. Karin Chenoweth and Christina Theokas describe the unexpectedly successful school leaders they studied as having to weigh "factors that non-experts may not even realize exist but that often make the difference between successful schools and mediocre ones." You call that easy? Sounds like rocket science to me, and that is just one person's job.

Then you have the teachers. Their jobs are equally complex. If a school is to be great, its teachers must be great. They have to understand they are in a service profession, or, even better, recognize that they have been called to serve. They have to be expert instructors, committed to and adept at the requisite best practices of education. They have to genuinely love children, including the inevitable unlovable children, and to know about child development and learning and cognition. They have to be expert mediators, between kids, between parents and kids, between parents, between teachers, etc. They have to be improvisers, and performers, and counselors, and parents (they are after all *in loco parentis*; as noted in Chapter 8). And they have to be self-knowledgeable and socially and emotionally competent. They have to be reflective professionals who are aware of all of this and how it is or isn't manifested

> If a school is to be great, its teachers must be great.

in them. And they have to be utterly ethical and pro-social. And of course do all of this for modest compensation and little social status. Sounds like rocket science to me.

As the saying goes, when a wealthy arrogant business man asked a teacher condescendingly, "What do you make?" the teacher's answer was "I make a difference."

Potholes in the Road to Excellence

As we have seen already in this book, there are many potholes along the road to educational success. Of course, we have to start with motives and intentions. This is usually not a problem. As was stated at the outset of the book, the vast majority of educators are well and appropriately motivated – they come to education for the flourishing (academic and developmental) of students. Their motives are pure.

The potholes tend to come further down the pedagogical path. Even with the right motivations, they still may not "get it." As the saying goes, "the path to failure is littered with good intentions." Such intentions to serve students' best interests are necessary but are not enough to ensure success.

Poor pre-professional preparation may send them off the path of success by not teaching them what good education is and what methods support the learning and development of students. Educators start way behind the eight ball in most cases because teacher preparation is often woefully inadequate. It is not that schools and colleges of education aren't trying (and I work in a College of Education). Rather, there are so many blocks to doing this well. Doing it well is rocket science. We often train educators with professors (and I am admittedly one of them) who don't or even can't do themselves what they are training the future teachers and administrators to do.

Part of the problem is that so much of teaching is an art and needs to be learned in the trenches of schools. But too often there is little quality control of what kinds of schools and classrooms student teachers observe. They need to see master teachers and best practices; too often they see burn out and mediocrity instead. I always tell new teachers that "You are not prepared to teach. Not because I know the college you attended but because rarely do I find any teachers who believe they were prepared to teach. Your best asset is the other teachers in your school. Find the best ones and build relationships with them. Seek out the best mentors; don't just take what you are given. Observe them and ask them to observe you. And be open to improvement. If you need others to simply affirm you, you are doomed."

> Part of the problem is that so much of teaching is an art and needs to be learned in the trenches of schools. But too often there is little quality control of what kinds of schools and classrooms student teachers observe.

Sometimes the pothole is that we don't know enough about what really works. This book is full of research-based recommendations for practice, but we still need to know much more.

There is too little funding for solid scientific research on effective education. Oftentimes funding for education is focused exclusively on implementation and only infrequently is there funding allotted to evaluate whether and why implementation works. When the funding is there for evaluation, it is often inadequate. Often it is wasted because those implementing don't know how to evaluate practice and fumble the evaluation ball. So much of federal funding for educational research is wasted for this reason. We desperately need a better culture to support the accumulation of scientific knowledge about effective education for all the purposes we discussed in Chapter 1.

As we noted in Chapter 5, educators may intuit best practices at home with their children and not see the application to school. That transfer from parenting to educating, or rather the lack of such transfer, is another potential pothole in this journey to great schooling.

In Chapter 11, we explored what great teaching is. Sometimes teachers know what great teaching is, but don't realize they aren't doing it. Peer observation, administrator observation, and guided reflection can help avoid this pothole. Indeed, even ascertaining when competency has been achieved is not easy.

I recall learning the hard way that there may be false victories in professional development. One principal who had lots of character education training, asked me to do a workshop for his staff before school started in the fall. Part of what I presented was a method for empowering the students to generate the behavioral norms for their classrooms for the year. The point was what I introduced as a "pedagogy of empowerment" in Chapter 10; that is, to authentically empower students to shape their classroom cultures. When I was done, the principal thanked me and told his staff that he really liked the idea of student-generated norms and then said "Besides, you can always change the students' words and ideas to fit whatever you want." Even after all that training, he simply did not "get it." In fact, simply "getting it" is high on my list of goals for educators.

On another occasion I went to watch a teacher whom we had trained as she trained her peers in class meeting skills. She did a wonderful training session, expressing a deep understanding of the concepts and practices. I was sure she really had mastered this stuff. Then I watched her lead a class meeting with her own class. It was way off target: authoritarian, teacher-dominated, a series of dialogues between her and different students, etc. That was when I realized that rhetorical understanding does not ensure practical understanding. The path from expert knowledge to effective practice is long, circuitous and complex. It is rocket science. Anyone who wants to change teacher practice has to recognize this in advance and plan accordingly.

For other educators, they may even know what great teaching is, realize they are falling short, but not know how to improve. Yet another potential pothole. When we do know what actually works (for example, we know that effective teachers love their students and love their subject matter), we rarely allot the necessary resources (money, leave time, professional development, etc.) to ensure that educators learn how to implement those practices. Federal and state priorities frequently push budgets and policies toward narrow agendas and leave no resources for that which is necessary for true school improvement. To make matters worse, so much of professional development in schools is unsystematic, unsustained, and often described as "faddish." Teachers ask for professional development to focus on core school improvement goals, to be sustained long enough to transform practice, and to be of high quality. Rarely is that the actual case. Along with professional development, quality mentoring, coaching, and the creation of a professional caring learning community (Chapter 17) can also help us avoid the pothole of not knowing how to improve our practice.

In St. Louis, we are blessed to have the best regional professional development resource I know of: CHARACTER*plus* (www.characterplus.org). It is a not-for-profit that is part of a cooperative of school districts. Its sole purpose is to provide the resources for schools and districts to implement quality character education, and is a large part of the reason so many schools in this region are excelling. This model of a regional professional development resource is not new, but its focus on character education is.

It is the inherent complexity of excellent education that really concerns me in this chapter. The stereotype that education is glorified baby-sitting and hence "not rocket science" only makes it more difficult for educators to master the complexity and challenges of their craft. Know that teaching kids is tough stuff, not because of the kids, but because of the nature of teaching. It is complex and difficult to understand and to master. Not just in education, but in life we often think that sheer willpower or desire is enough to get us through when we are trying to smooth out the rough edges on ourselves or to motivate others to do so.

I frequently hear principals claim that "all the teachers in my school will be positive role models." Nice goal. How are you going to do that? Got a plan? As noted in Chapter 11, I like to ask principals more generally "What are you doing every day to make each teacher in your school the best teacher he or she can be?" Dreaming it is a lot easier than accomplishing it. You should be grappling and struggling as you try to become the best teacher you can be. Have I mentioned that it is rocket science?

Five Big Lessons Learned from Rats and Kids and Schools

Rats have gotten a bad rap. Sure they were instrumental in killing an estimated 25 million people in Europe and Asia in the Black Plague, a series of pandemics spanning 15 centuries. But that is over now; long past the time to forgive and forget. And sure they are ugly and frightening and dirty and vicious, but so are some people I know. They are also intrepid and resourceful and adaptable and resilient...all character strengths! And where would modern psychology be without rats running through mazes and getting shocked (see how unfairly we treat them?)? But I come to bury this rat, not to praise him, even if I owe him a great debt. For this book probably would not have been written if it weren't for my parable of the child and his brother's pet rat. (By the way, if you are starting this book from the back, you deserve the confusion you are now experiencing).

If on the other hand, you have earned reading this summation chapter by having read the entire book, then I thank you and congratulate you. And I sincerely hope you have found it worth your while. It was a labor of love; love for the students that you teach and love for teachers who you work with, supervise, or simply care about. You likely have noticed that I typically try to explain why teachers sometimes do some odd (and often counterproductive) things. I see our teacher training systems failing them. I see the national organizational structure of education failing them. I have often seen school boards and teacher unions impeding good education. But I attribute to them hearts of gold. I truly believe that most educators sincerely care deeply about children. I wouldn't bother doing the work I do if I thought otherwise.

As I hope I have made clear repeatedly, I am in this for the kids. As a developmental psychologist, my eye is on what is in the best developmental interests of children and adolescents. And schools are powerful players in the nurturing of child development. I am simply trying to get schools to understand and implement that which best serves students' learning and development. My concern is that educators *want* to do this, but often don't seem to know *how* to do this. And that is the crux of this book. So let's close it out by looking back at some of the key lessons learned. However, I do not mean the following to be an exhaustive summary of *all* the lessons learned in it; merely a highlighting of some key themes. In other words, if you are actually starting this book here, this summary won't suffice; you are just going to have go back and read it from the beginning.

FIVE BIG LESSONS

Lesson One: Knowing, naming, and living your purpose. It is the purpose of schools to foster the positive development of youth including their moral character and civic character, along with their learning and academic growth.

Lesson Two: Good education *is* rocket science. Whereas understanding the purpose of schooling is tough stuff, actually building and living a school based on those understandings is even harder.

Lesson Three: Schools are for kids. In order to transform schools to be more effective at both academics and character formation, we need to understand and love kids.

Lesson Four: Adults have awesome power over children. We need to do a better job of recognizing and then harnessing the awesome power of the adults in the school to influence student learning and development.

Lesson Five: Schools are complex social organizations. Schools are social organizations, and as such we need to think about them as communities and as systems of relationships, and about how power is distributed in schools.

The Big Picture: Five Big Lessons

In the journey that is this book, we have made many stops as we traveled through the 20 chapters, numerous stories, and various attempts at catalyzing epiphanies. In a way of summing up, I want to close with five clusters of lessons learned: what I am calling the *Five Big Lessons.*

LESSON ONE: Knowing, naming, and living your purpose. One of the most important points of this book is that it is the purpose of schools to foster the positive development of youth including their moral character and civic character, along with their learning and academic growth, and furthermore that it is unavoidable. The promotion of such development in schools helps schools teach more effectively and fulfills the fundamental developmental purpose of schools as well.

Schools and educators often don't understand that obligation and interplay. Even if they do, they frequently do not know what is actually in the best interests of student learning and development. It is crucial to know the purposes of your school, to codify them in your seminal purpose statements (mission, vision, values, touchstone), and to use them to drive policy and practice. They need to be more than merely "words on the wall"...indeed, much more.

LESSON TWO: Good education *is* rocket science. Whereas understanding the purpose of schooling is tough stuff, actually building and living a school based on those understandings is even harder. *Character education, indeed all high quality education, is rocket science.* It is not easy to understand, master, or implement.

Part of the challenge is to be a reflective practitioner and therefore to know what you do. And what you do actually does...for and to kids. One also has to be a critically reflective practitioner so that you can separate the wheat from the chaff. You have to know what works and then master and implement what works, and you must be willing to change not just what you do but who you are as an educator. For example, if the goal of education is to get students to internalize good values, then we must avoid extrinsic motivators and rely on practices that promote the internalization of values so that they become enduring motivators.

A related theme is represented by my repeated use of the term "strategic and intentional." Even when we recognize the need for certain educational reforms, we often think that they will just happen. I have seen administrators repeatedly gravitate toward the notion of all teachers as role models for student learning and character development, and then never question how to strategically and intentionally make it happen. Rather they seem to naively and likely unconsciously assume that it will just happen by the mere fact of them wanting it to be so. We can't just embrace or endorse best practices and school reform; rather, we have to strategically and intentionally ensure that they are happening.

This is especially poignant given all the "bad pedagogical habits" I have chronicled throughout the book. Beyond intentionally putting into practice good strategies and policies, we have to first become aware of and then cease the harmful or ineffective practices that exist so frequently. Putting a disproportionate amount of time and energy into the *golden children* who need us much less to make it in life than do the *tarnished children* who we ignore or even marginalize or vilify. And the ways we simply squander the immense intellectual and creative capacity of all stakeholders in the school, even those adorable four- and five-year-olds in your early childhood and kindergarten classrooms, but also the teachers and support staff and others who have a vested interest in the school's success but little power to support and improve it.

LESSON THREE: Schools are for kids. We often hear the terms "child-centered" or "student-centered" in discussions of quality, effective education. That has been a recurrent theme in this book. In order to transform schools to be more effective at both academics and character formation, we need to understand and love kids.

The rat that was the focus of this book teaches us that kids don't jettison their lives at the school door; rather they bring them with them into your classrooms and you need to accept that and deal with it, rather than ignoring it or asking kids to simply forget what is so pressing and salient to them.

Furthermore, from the parenting and educational research literature we learned how important it is to love kids both for their learning and their development. They have to be the cherished focus of classrooms and schools. Remember, "kids don't care how much you know, until they know how much you care." And you won't fool them for long.

Teaching is a calling to service to children. That puts them front and center and underscores their value.

LESSON FOUR: Adults have awesome power over children. We need to do a better job of recognizing and then harnessing the awesome power of the adults in the school to influence student learning and development. Unless we do, we have essentially set a very low ceiling on how successful we can ever be.

The analogy between parenting and teaching is one way we can better understand and harness the power of adults in schools to support student flourishing. We know so much about which parent behaviors positively impact kids and we now know that such behaviors also promote learning and development across the preK–12 educational spectrum.

One of the more specific ways we explored the power of educators, and for that matter all adults who interact with children, is through the power of role-modeling. We must be the character we want to see in our students. We need to recognize the impact of our behaviors and of our selves on students, and use that for the good.

Another way to harness the power of adults is through the power of their words. What we say matters...deeply. So we need to mind our tongues. We need to speak in ways and with words that will nurture and heal, not in ways that will hurt and destroy.

LESSON FIVE: Schools are complex social organizations. To truly improve schools and do the best we can in educating and developmentally nurturing students, we have to be sociologists. (Like I said...it *is* rocket science.) Schools are social organizations, and as such we need to think about them as communities and as systems of relationships, and about how power is distributed in schools.

A theme throughout this book has been that one key purpose of schools, at least in democratic societies, is the nurturing of the next generation of citizens who understand, are motivated to, and have the capacities to engage in the democratic process to promote the common good. We have noted how hierarchical and authoritarian schools tend to be, even when the intentions of those in power (superintendents, principals, teachers, etc.) are loving. A benevolent dictatorship is still a dictatorship.

So a *pedagogy of empowerment* needs to be nurtured in our classrooms and schools. And that includes enabling productive dissent. In all of this, the invitation of voices, the creation of places for voices to be heard, and the authentic consideration of voices are crucial. Class meetings, authentic student government, and servant leadership are some examples of ways of doing this.

Leadership is key to successful schools, and hence to rethinking the governance structure of schools. Rarely does a school achieve excellence without an excellent leader. Part of that excellence is understanding the importance of, and shepherding the improvement of, the adult culture in the school.

A Final Word

So I want to end with a final word about a specific virtue...namely, courage. It takes a lot to confront, accept, and deploy whatever wisdom you cull from this book. Those educators named in these pages that I hold up as role models deserve all of our respect for their courage, their wisdom, their intelligence, and their pure hearts. The Amy Johnstons, the Phil Vincents, the Hal Urbans, the Karen Smiths, the Kristen Pelsters, the Tim Crutchleys, the Jennifer Diekens, the Ron Bergers, the Avis Glazes, the Charles Elbots, the Sheldon Bermans, the Cynthia Whitakers, the Linda Rayfords, the Laura Eckens, the Beverly Nances, the Bob Hassingers, the Jennifer Rephs, the Gus Jacobs of the world. They make it happen. They are doing what we all need to do. They care about kids, understand the power of schools, doggedly pursue what is excellence in education, and have creatively each found a unique path to create great schools that foster the development of great students and future citizens of our society. And that is a sacred task and trust.

I have learned so much from all of them. I hope that I have been able to pay it forward.

Books Cited

Abourjilie, C. (2000). *Developing Character for Classroom Success: Strategies to Increase Responsibility, Achievement, and Motivation in Secondary Students.* Chapel Hill, NC: Character Development Publishing.

Argyris, C., & Schon, D.A. (1977). *Theory in practice: Increasing professional effectiveness.* San Francisco: Jossey-Bass.

Berger, R. *An Ethic of Excellence: Building a Culture of Craftsmanship in Schools.* Portsmouth, NH: Heinemann.

Character Education Partnership. *Performance Values: Why They Matter and What Schools Can Do to Foster Their Development*

Chenoweth, K., & Theokas, C. *Getting it Done: Leading Academic Success in Unexpected Schools.* Cambridge MA: Harvard Education Press.

Collins, J. (2001). *Good to Great: Why Some Companies Make the Leap...and Others Don't.* New York: HarperCollins.

Cooper, D., & Cooper, K. (2012). *J4 Learning: How to Create Training for the Digital Age.* St. Louis: TotalComm Press.

Deci, E. L., & Ryan, R. M. (2002). *Handbook of self-determination research.* Rochester, NY: University of Rochester Press

Developmental Studies Center (1996). *Ways we want our class to be: Class meetings that build commitment to kindness and learning.* Oakland CA: Developmental Studies Center.

DuFour, R. & Eaker, R. (1998). *Professional Learning Communities at Work: Best Practices for Enhancing Student Achievement.* Alexandria VA: Association for Supervision and Curriculum Development.

Elbot, C.F., & Fulton, D. (2008). *Building an Intentional School Culture: Excellence in Academics and Character.* Thousand Oaks, CA: Corwin.

Erwin, J.C. (2004). *The Classroom of Choice: Giving Students What They Need and Getting What You Want.* Alexandria VA: Association for Supervision and Curriculum Development.

Fisher, R.S., Henry, E., & Porter, D. (2006). *Morning Meeting Messages: 180 Sample Charts from Three Classrooms.* Turners Falls, MA: Northeast Foundation for Children.

Frankl, V. (1971). *Man's Search for Meaning: An Introduction to Logotherapy.* New York: Pocket Books.

Gardner, H. (1993). *Frames of Mind: The Theory of multiple intelligences.* New York: Basic Books.

Glasser, W. (1969). *Schools without failure.* New York: Harper and Row.

Greenleaf, R.K. (2008). *The Servant Leader.* Westfield IN: The Greenleaf Center for Servant Leadership.

Jackson, P.W., Boostrom, R.E., & Hansen, D.T. (1993). *The moral life of schools.* San Francisco: Jossey Bass.

Johnstone, K. (). *Impro: Improvisation and the theatre.* New York: Routledge

Kohn, A. (1995). *Punished by Rewards: The Trouble with Gold Stars, Incentive Plans, A's, Praise and Other Bribes.* New York: Mariner Books.

Kriete, R. (2002). *The Morning Meeting Book.* Greenfield, MA: Northeast Foundation for Children.

Lickona, T. (1983). *Raising good children: Helping your child through the stages of moral development—From birth through the teenage years.* New York: Bantam Books.

Lickona, T. (1991) *Educating for character: How our schools can teach respect and responsibility.* New York: Bantam Books.

Lickona, T. (2004). *Character matters: How to help our children develop good judgment, integrity, and other essential virtues.* New York: Simon and Schuster.

Lickona, T., & Davidson, M. (2005). *Smart and Good High Schools.* Washington DC: Character Education Partnership.

Palmer, Parker J. (1998). *The courage to teach: Exploring the inner landscape of a teacher's life.* San Francisco: Jossey-Bass.

Power, F.C., Higgins, A., & Kohlberg, L. (1989). *Lawrence Kohlberg's Approach to Moral Education.* New York: Columbia University Press.

Ravitch, D. (2010). *The Death and Life of the Great American School System: How Testing and Choice are Undermining Education.* New York: Basic Books.

Seligman, M.E.P. (2012). *Flourish: A visionary new understanding of happiness and well-being.* New York: Free Press.

Sizer, T.R., & Sizer, N.F. (1999). *The students are watching: Schools and the moral contract.* Boston: Beacon Press.

Streight, D. (2008). *Parenting for Character: Five Experts, Five Practices.* Portland: The Council for Spiritual and Ethical Education.

Taulbert, C.L. (1997). *Eight habits of the heart: Timeless values that build strong communities—Within our homes and our lives.* New York: Penguin Books.

Tucker, M.C. & Darling-Hammond, L. (2011). *Surpassing Shanghai: An Agenda for American Education Built on the World's Leading Systems.* Cambridge MA: Harvard Education Press.

Urban, H. (2003). *Life's Greatest Lessons: 20 Things that Matter.* New York: Fireside Press.

Urban, H. (2008). *Lessons from the Classroom: 20 Things Good Teachers Do.* Redwood City, CA: Great Lessons Press.

Vincent, P.F. (2006). *Restoring School Civility: Creating a Caring, Responsible, and Productive School.* Chapel Hill NC: Character Development Group.

Wagner, T., & Kegan, R. (2006). *Change Leadership: A Practical Guide to Transforming Our Schools.* San Francisco: Jossey-Bass.

Watson, M. (2003). *Learning to Trust: Transforming Difficult Elementary Classrooms Through Developmental Discipline.* San Francisco: Jossey-Bass.

Websites Cited

Building Community Institute: www.cliftontaulbert.com

Center for Character and Citizenship: www.characterandcitizenship.org

Center for the 4th and 5th Rs: www2.cortland.edu/centers/character

Character Development Group: www.charactereducation.com

Character Education Partnership:www.character.org

CHARACTER*plus*: www.characterplus.org

Center for Spiritual and Ethical Education: www.csee.org

Collaborative for Academic, Social and Emotional Learning: www.casel.org

ComedySportz: www.comedysportz.com

Developmental Studies Center: www.devstu.org

Edu-quest International: www.avisglaze.ca

Giraffe Project: www.giraffe.org

Greenleaf Center for Servant Leadership: www.greenleaf.org

Institute for Excellence & Ethics: excellenceandethics.com

Institute of Moralogy: www.moralogy.jp/english/MORALOGY.PDF

International Center for Academic Integrity: http://www.academicintegrity.org

National School Climate Center: www.schoolclimate.org

Open Circle: www.open-circle.org

Search Institute: http://www.search-institute.org/

Self-Determination Theory: http://www.psych.rochester.edu/SDT/

Teaching Tolerance: www.tolerance.org

The Responsive Classroom: www.responsiveclassroom.org

About the Author

Dr. Marvin W. Berkowitz is the inaugural Sanford N. McDonnell Endowed Professor of Character Education, and co-director of the Center for Character and Citizenship at the University of Missouri–St. Louis, and University of Missouri President's Thomas Jefferson Professor. He has also served as the inaugural Ambassador H.H. Coors Professor of Character Development at the U.S. Air Force Academy (1999), and professor of psychology and director of the Center for Ethics Studies at Marquette University (1979–1999). He was also founder and associate director of the Center for Addiction and Behavioral Health Research in Milwaukee.

Born in Queens, New York, in 1950, he earned his BA degree in psychology from the State University of New York at Buffalo in 1972, and his Ph.D. in Life-span Developmental Psychology at Wayne State University in 1977. He served as a research associate at the Center for Moral Development and Education at Harvard University 1977–79. He has served as a visiting scholar in Canada, Germany, Switzerland, Scotland, Spain, and Taiwan.

His scholarly focus and expertise is in character education and development. He is author of *Parenting for Good* (2005), editor of *Moral Education: Theory and Application* (1985) and *Peer Conflict and Psychological Growth* (1985), and author of more than 100 book chapters, monographs, and journal articles. He is founding co-editor of the *Journal for Research in Character Education*.

Dr. Berkowitz was named "Outstanding Young Educator of 1983" by the Milwaukee Jaycees, was cited as one of Milwaukee's "87 Most Interesting People" in *Milwaukee* magazine (1987), named "Best University Professor" in a 1998 readers' poll of the *Shepherd's Express*, was named Educator of the Year by the St. Louis Association of Secondary School Principals (2005), was an inaugural recipient of the Bill Porzukowiak Character Award (2005), received the Sanford N. McDonnell Lifetime Achievement Award from the Character Education Partnership (2006), the first Exemplary Partner Award from the Charmm'd Foundation (2008), the Good Works Award from the Association for Moral Education (2010), and the University of Missouri System's Thomas Jefferson Professorship (2011).

He is co-founder of ComedySportz, a nationally franchised improvisational comedy show, and has co-written the play "Chuck, Bob, and Louie" which won best of show at the 1994 Milwaukee Festival of 10-Minute Plays. For five years he was author of a weekly newspaper column on parenting for character published in the *Topeka (KS) Capitol-Journal*. He is also a two-time Missouri State Senior Division Soccer gold medalist (2006, 2007). He has been married to Judith Gewanter Berkowitz for nearly 40 years and has one son, Daniel William Berkowitz.